First English Language Edition of

The Dossier of Subject № 1218

A Bulgarian Anarchist's Story

by **Alexander Nakov**

TARGETED FOR HIS HOSTILITY TO THE PEOPLE'S STATE

Translated from the Bulgarian original by **Mariya Radeva**

Edited by **Rob Blow**

Foreword by **Nick Heath**

Black Cat Press
Edmonton, Alberta

The Dossier of Subject Nº 1218
A Bulgarian Anarchist's Story
by **Alexander Nakov**

Translated from the Bulgarian original by **Mariya Radeva**
Edited by **Rob Blow**
Foreword by **Nick Heath**

Library and Archives Canada Cataloguing in Publication

Nakov, Aleksand˘ur Metodiev
[Dosie na obekt No 1218. English]
   The dossier of subject no 1218 : a Bulgarian anarchist's story /
by Alexander Nakov, targeted for his hostility to the people's state ;
translated from the Bulgarian original by Mariya Radeva ; edited by
Rob Blow ; foreword by Nick Heath. -- First English language edition.

   Includes index.
   Translation of: Dosie na obekt No 1218.
   ISBN 978-1-926878-16-4 (paperback)

   1. Nakov, Aleksand˘ur Metodiev. 2. Political prisoners-
-Bulgaria-- Biography. 3. Anarchists--Bulgaria--Biography.
4. Political persecution-- Bulgaria. 5. Bulgaria--Politics and
government--1944-1990. I. Blow, Rob, 961-, editor II. Title.

   DR93.N35A3 2016   949.903'1092   C2016-901284-0

Printed and published by:

4508 118 Avenue
Edmonton, Alberta
Canada T5W 1A9
www.blackcatpress.ca

Contents

Photos and other graphics used:

During 2009, a commemorative exhibition entitled "Without a Trace? The Labor Camp in Belene 1949-1959 and Afterward..." was on display, in Bulgaria, at Sofia's National Art Gallery. Among other items were reconstructions of the Belene camp by survivor and cartographer Krum Horozov. Samples of his work are found on pages 54-56. Also on display were photos taken by Mikhail Daskalov, a soldier stationed at the Belene camp on Persin Island in the 1940s. The upper photo on the front cover from Daskalov shows dirt being moved by cart at a dike on the island. The complete catalogue for the display can be found here: *http:// minaloto.org/index.php?option=com_content&view=article&id=390:wi thout-a-trace-the-labour-camp-in-belene-1949-1959-&catid=25:books- and-collections&Itemid=37.*

The photo of Alexander Nakov on the back cover is from the photo gallery of Ekaterina Yosifova, Bulgarian journalist and poet, at: *http://libkustendil. primasoft.bg/html/bibliografia_eyo/galeria.htm.*

Graphics from the Pernik State Archives (Dŭrzhaven arkhiv - Pernik): front cover (lower left): Alexander Nakov as a soldier with young people of Kosacha in 1940 (ДА – Перник, Ф. 1144, оп. 1, а.е. 16, л.); p. 2: map of state mines of Pernik from Ts. Brŭshlyanov, "State Mines of Pernik" (1928), p. 37; p. 5 (ДА – Перник, Ф. 1144, оп. 1, а.е. 16, л. 2); p. 123 (ДА – Перник, Ф. 1144, оп. 1, а.е. 17, л. 2).

Images used with the permission of the original Bulgarian publisher, IC 'Shrapnel' in Sofia are found on the title page and pages xxviii, 7, 12, 62, 79, 81, 87, 95, 113, 126, 127, 129, 131, 135, and 137.

Images from Alexander Nakov's private collection are found on pages 3,11,41, 96, 100, 101, and 116.

The photo on page 124 is used with the permission of Dimitrije Janičić.

The map of Bulgaria on page xviii is from the Perry-Castañeda Library Map Collection at the University of Texas (*http://www.lib.utexas.edu/ maps/bulgaria.html*).

The map of Bulgaria on page 53 is by the Bulgarian cartographer Plamen (*https://goo.gl/2xtZJ4*).

The map of the region around Kosacha on page 125 is provided by the Bulgarian cartographer Ikonact (*https://commons.wikimedia.org/wiki/ User:Ikonact*).

Editor's Acknowledgements

Special thanks go to Viola M. Ando in Japan for bringing Alexander, Mariya and me together to work on this project and to Mariya Radeva, not only for her work in translating the text but for all her running to and fro between Alexander, various third parties in Bulgaria and the editor in the UK. A big thank you also goes to Nick Heath for providing us with his historical overview of the Bulgarian movement. Thank you to Maria Bragoli, Neil Skinner and Todor Ivanov for their invaluable advice and assistance; to Georgi Konstantinov at IK 'Shrapnel' for the original text; to everyone at the Kate Sharpley Library, particularly Paul Sharkey, for the already translated document from the archives of the Bulgarian State Security; to Nestor McNab for the translation of the 1945 FACB Platform and to Dimitrije Janičić for the photos of Alexander at SAT Congress. Finally, extra special thanks go to Alexander Nakov himself for his story, his life and for his steadfast example to us all.

Rob Blow

Bibliographical Information

Alexander Nakov, Dossier of Subject No.1218: A Bulgarian Anarchist's Story. First English edition translated in 2012 by Mariya Radeva and edited by Rob Blow, 2013, from: Nakov, Alexander, (2009), **Dossier of Subject No. 1218**, 2nd ed., Sofia: IK 'Shrapnel' / Александър Наков, (2009), **Досие на обект, №1218**, ИК „Шрапнел" (София: 2009). First Bulgarian edition published in 2006 by IK 'Shrapnel,' Sofia.

Second revised and complete Bulgarian edition published in 2009 to mark the author's 90th birthday.

FOREWORD

BY NICK HEATH

A Historical Background to the Bulgarian Anarchist Movement

The Bulgarian anarchist movement has produced many heroic figures, not least Alexander Nakov himself, but there were many others. Georgi Sheytanov* comes to mind, as do Dimitar Balkhov, Stanko Paraskov and a host of others. Georgi Balkanski (real name Grigoriev), who became the historian of the movement and helped publicize it in the West, was himself an exceptional activist within the movement.

Hristo Botev, elevated to the stature of 'National Poet' by the Stalinist regime and still held in great esteem in Bulgaria, was to fall under the influence of the Russian anarchist Mikhail Bakunin and was probably the first to introduce anarchist ideas into Bulgaria with his distribution of Bakunin's **Statism and Anarchy** there. He founded the first Bulgarian libertarian group at Brăila, across the border in Romania.

In the decades to come and after the independence of Bulgaria from the Ottoman Empire was established in 1877, socialist and libertarian propaganda began to be spread within the country. Spiro Gulapchev established the first socialist publishing house, Skoropechatnitsa (Rapid Printing) at Ruse. Most of the contributors were anarchists, with a number of Marxist writers also contributing. Among the libertarian contributors were Nicolai Stoinov, Varban Kilifarski and Paraskev Stoyanov (the founder of surgery in Bulgaria).

Stoinov and Kilifarski helped form the first peasant unions in Bulgaria and Stoinov also participated in the founding of the Union of Teachers, the first union in Bulgaria, in July 1895. Kilifarski and Stoinov founded the Bezvlastie (Acracia -

---
*Alternative spelling, Cheitanov.

Hristo Botev   Georgi Sheytanov   Vasil Ikonomov

no rule) publishing house in 1908 which published all the
essential texts of anarchism. This allowed the greater spread
of libertarian ideas so that by 1910, there was already talk of
an anarchist federation to coordinate the activities of local
groups.

Mikhail Gerdzhikov founded the paper *Probuda* (Awakening) in 1912 with the aim of organizing the nascent movement.
Two years later, other anarchist publications appeared: the
paper *Rabotnikcheska Missal* (Workers' Thought) and the
magazine *Osvobodenye* (Liberation). The Ruse group at-
tempted to set up an anarcho-syndicalist movement with a
programme and aims and principles and set up a publishing
house of the same name.

The wars in the Balkans and the First World War brought
anarchist publishing activity to a halt. However, the number
of people refusing military service grew considerably. This
period was characterized by bold acts of armed struggle by
some anarchists, epitomised by the dashing and romantic
revolutionary, Georgi Sheytanov. They proved to be a serious
threat to the State. The amount of propaganda increased in
volume. It was indicative of the development of the movement that Sheytanov turned away from armed action towards
the building of a mass movement.

Rabotnicheska Missal reappeared in 1919 and took the

initiative to call for the founding conference of an anarchist federation. This took place in Sofia between 15th and 17th June where more than 150 delegates from different towns and villages attended. The congress decided to establish The Anarchist Communist Federation of Bulgaria (FACB). A large number of groups were now formed in nearly all towns and the biggest villages. The movement attracted workers, students and high school students, as well as teachers, white collar workers and various professionals. Many conferences and meetings took place and **Probuda** became the official organ of the FACB.

When it was closed down by the authorities, underground and other still legally published papers took its place. The next three conferences of the FACB took place in secret. Finally a legal conference took place at Yambol in 1923, attended by 104 delegates and 350 observers representing 89 local groupings. The conference reported that **Rabotnicheska Missal** had a print run of 7,500 copies, distributed in 140 localities. There were four publishing houses and 16 pamphlets had been published in this period. The conference attracted the attention of the authorities and subsequent repression, resulting in the murder of 30 anarchists by the authorities on March 26 1923 and a subsequent military coup on June 9. Subsequent risings in September were bloodily put down.

The establishment of a repressive regime with the King at its head led eventually in 1926 to the setting up of a 'democratic' government, which gave the anarchist movement a little leeway and allowed for the publication of several papers and magazines. However, the movement as a whole still had to exist underground and was only able to hold one national congress in secret at Kazanlik in August 1927. Because of the difficulties of illegality and the repressive regime, there were problems of disorganization in this period. This prompted moves towards greater organization within the FACB. Bulgarian anarchism had always rejected individualism and revolutionary syndicalism and above all defined itself as anarchist communist, citing Bakunin, Kropotkin, Malatesta, Faure, etc. Anarcho-syndicalism remained a minor current within Bulgaria. At the same time, the Bulgarian anarchists prioritized the creation of workers' and peasants' organizations.

Partisans of the Organizational Platform of the Libertarian Communists, written by the Ukrainian and Russian anarchists Makhno, Arshinov, Mett and others, now had a certain popularity in Bulgaria. There was a resulting clash within the movement. The majority of the FACB remained tied to traditional concepts of anarchist communism, expressed through the organization of the FACB. The clash between the traditionalists and the Platformists became quite bitter, causing splits within the movement.

Meanwhile, a quite considerable number of anarchist militants established themselves in southern France and in Paris. They supplied support to the comrades back home, while at the same time formulating a new platform and programme for the FACB. These exiles returned to Bulgaria following an amnesty and worked towards the convening of a secret conference in a forest near Lovech. This was attended by 90 delegates. Unanimity was achieved, the papers of the two different tendencies were suspended, and *Rabotnicheska Missal* was established as the united paper of the FACB. However, the principal advocates of the Platform violently disagreed with this, which led to widespread disapproval within the movement and the rapid disappearance of this grouping. The pure syndicalists, sceptical of a specificly anarchist organization, also withdrew from the FACB after several months.

A follow-up conference held secretly in the mountains near Maglizh affirmed the need for a specific organization, for tactical and ideological unity, and for a programme of action. Local groups federated into five regional organizations within the FACB.

As well as consistent propaganda, the FACB developed everyday agitation among workers and peasants with organizational work, the establishment of cooperatives, cultural groups, free schools and libraries. This period of relative liberty nevertheless involved the arrest of militants and the closing down of publications. Another coup took place on 19th May 1934 and the movement once more had to go underground. There was support for the Spanish Revolution in 1936 with 30 comrades managing to get to Spain. The dictatorship and the subsequent period of Nazism during World War II limited much activity. The Bulgarian Communist Party itself, whilst also underground, had no liking for anarchists, as witnessed by its murder of the anarchist resistance fighter and agronomist Radko Kaitazov, on the day of the liberation from Nazism in 1944.

This was a herald of what was to come: a new Stalinist regime, carried through by a military coup with the support of the Soviet Army, which took place on 9th September 1944. For a while the legal existence of the anarchist movement was possible, allowing the holding of a conference in October of that year in Sofia. *Rabotnicheska Missal* was once again published for four issues before it was shut down again by the authorities. The activities of local groups continued, leading to a well-organized secret conference on 10th March 1945 near Sofia. It was attended by 90 delegates. However, the secret police conducted a raid and arrested all the delegates, who were then placed in a concentration camp. Fortunately, circumstances within the new Stalinist regime led to their liberation and the publishing of four issues of the paper. The print run shot up from 7,000 to 30,000, and if there had not been paper rationing, there would have been printed 60,000! However, the occupying Red Army subsequently suspended the paper because its soldiers were reading it and were starting to come under the influence of anarchism.

The regime now instituted a new period of repression, with anarchists being interned in concentration camps. Another secret conference took place in Sofia in August 1946, with 400 groups represented. An underground duplicated bulletin replaced the banned FACB paper. A further wave of repression was carried out in December 1948, two days before the fifth congress of the Communist Party. More than 600 anarchists were arrested and detained in concentration camps. Many militants escaped abroad, the exodus starting in 1946 and continuing up until 1951. These militants established the Bulgarian Anarchist Union in exile, working within the anarchist international organizations of the International Workers Association (IWA-AIT) and the International of Anarchist Federations (IAF-IFA).

With the fall of the different Stalinist regimes throughout Eastern Europe, the Bulgarian anarchist movement re-emerged from clandestinity and established the Bulgarian Anarchist Federation (FAB), which exists to this day.

The history of the anarchist movement in Bulgaria is one marked by great heroism, of fevered propaganda and activity, often under very difficult circumstances. Bulgaria was one of the countries where anarchism developed outside of small groupings to become a large movement. It deserves far more attention than it has received in the past. The publication of this book on the life of the exemplary anarchist militant, Alexander Nakov, is hopefully the beginning of a re-evaluation of that movement.

INTRODUCTION

BY ROB BLOW

Alexander Nakov's story is a truly remarkable one, spanning a broad sweep of 20th and 21st century history. Since his youthful political awakening, inspired by the Spanish Revolution in the heady days of 1936, right through to the present, at 94 years of age, he remains fully committed to the anarchist cause.

What is also remarkable is the fact that Alexander earned his anarchist spurs the hard way. He recently told the translator of this volume, Mariya Radeva, that he was born in 1919, received his secondary education in fascist prisons, and gained his higher education in Bolshevik prisons. In one sense, he is making light of his past with his characteristic dry humour, but make no mistake, his is a past filled with pain, tragedy and unspeakable cruelty. Nevertheless, the brutality of their Stalinist tormentors in places such as the notorious Belene concentration camp was met with the everyday solidarity, comradeship and mutual aid practised among the anarchist prisoners there. In this way, Alexander provides us with an account that is filled with hope, despite the horror of the situation.

However, Alexander Nakov is known for his modesty and would probably say that his story is also unremarkable in the context of Bulgaria's historic anarchist movement[*] and the severity of its repression by the ultra-orthodox, arch-Stalinist Bulgarian Communist Party (BCP), and under the monarcho-fascist regime before it. With this in mind then, we understand that Alexander is one of countless comrades forced to endure such barbarity from the so-called People's State.

---

[*]Although at Pernik's state archive, which holds an extensive personal historical record for Alexander Nakov, he is referred to as "one of the most famous Bulgarian anarchists."

One point that immediately strikes the reader is the sheer scale of Bulgaria's anarchist movement in the mid-20th century. This was clearly no minority political grouping operating on the fringes of society but, under the wing of the Federation of Anarchist Communists in Bulgaria (FACB), among other libertarian organizations, it was a sizable and well-organized social and political movement. Deeply entrenched in town and village life, it was a movement that often outshone its Bolshevik antagonists.

As the Bolshevik regimes, Bulgaria included, began to topple one-by-one, and the FACB re-established itself as the Federation of Anarchists in Bulgaria (FAB), it is interesting to note the composition of the early FAB as a mix of young people, new to anarchism, and those veteran survivors of fascist prisons and Bolshevik concentration camps. Alexander provides us with a detailed record of the FAB's Founding Conference, and in reading this document, one recognizes a cautious meld between old and young, reaching across the generations to found a new movement. While western European or North American anarchists may have criticisms of certain elements of their Founding Resolution, we should bear in mind that this statement by the FAB was drawn up at the end of 45 repressive years of Stalinist darkness, when our comrades were still tentatively feeling their way towards the light.

Yet, although a mass movement, historic Bulgarian anarchism still remains relatively unknown in the English-speaking anarchist scene. Notable exceptions to this are the pamphlet, ***Bulgaria, the New Spain,***[*] the online article, *The Anarchist-Communist Mass Line: Bulgarian Anarchism Armed*, by Michael Schmidt and Jack Grancharoff,[†] as well as several online vignettes of little-known anarchists, viewable on the

---

[*]Originally published in 1948 by the Alexander Berkman Aid Fund in Chicago, reprinted in the early 1980s by Terry Liddle's Kulak Press (London), and, more recently, by Zabalaza Books in South Africa.

[†]Viewable at **anarkismo.net**.

websites of the Kate Sharpley Library and Libcom.* Much
of this information was often thanks to and based on the
work of the Paris-based Bulgarian Libertarian Union in exile
(ULB). However, beyond the anarchist movement, in other
words, looking at the world of academic historians, journalists, and experts in the politics of Eastern Europe and the
former Soviet Bloc, Bulgarian anarchism has been noticeably
neglected. This has been to such an extent that it is as if the
mass Bulgarian anarchist movement simply never existed.

The possible reasons for this neglect are varied. Prior to
the collapse of the eastern European state capitalist systems,
both academic and journalistic interest has tended to be from
one of three political biases: the pro-Soviet left; the relatively
anti-Soviet left, or the virulently anti-Soviet right. The pro-
Soviet position was always that of enthusiastic cheerleader
for the Warsaw Pact countries and, understandably, had no
interest in raising the profile of their anarchist enemies.
The more critical left-wing position viewed these systems
as either deformed or degenerated workers' states, or even
went as far as labelling them state capitalist.† However, they
too had no interest in looking beyond the boundaries of their
Marxist-Leninist mind-set but instead, were more interested in promoting their own more or less orthodox brand of
Bolshevism, usually one of the 57 varieties of Trotskyism.
The right-wing anti-Soviet view, which rabidly promoted
liberal-democratic, laissez-faire capitalism, was only ever
interested in publicising 'pro-western' dissidents or assisting
groups such as the anti-Soviet Mujahedeen, forerunners of
the Taliban and Al Qaeda. And if the chosen dissidents were
not completely pro-west, then they would make damn sure
they were portrayed as such: 'anti-communist' rebels wanting
nothing more than to swap their own repressive regimes for
a US-style liberal-democracy, complete with a Big Mac and

---

*See www.katesharpleylibrary.net and libcom.org.
†This traditional anarchist view was also held by the UK Socialist
Workers' Party.

fries. Clearly, Bulgarian anarchism could never fit such a distorted bourgeois democratic pattern.

This is not to say there was simply a concerted anti-anarchist conspiracy between researchers, political analysts and journalists, whether from the left or right. Neither was the historical neglect of Bulgarian anarchism simply down to Cold War politics or a pro- or anti-Soviet tunnel-vision. It should also be understood that there are relatively few Bulgarian speakers outside of Bulgaria. Add to this, the then governing Bulgarian Communist Party's practice of keeping the population on an extremely tight leash, as well as carefully vetting and monitoring any information that left the country, then it is hardly surprising that quality information on the historic Bulgarian anarchist movement, outside of that provided by the ULB, has been hard to find.

One aim of this volume, then, is to go some way towards remedying the neglect of this significant part of the international anarchist movement. Alexander's book is important in that it is an authentic, first-hand account of this historic movement. He has been meticulous in listing the names of numerous comrades from his village, from other towns and cities and from prisons and camps. A few are still alive, but most are now long gone. In this way, the contribution of every comrade mentioned in this story is kept alive. Serving as the movement's memory, Alexander is helping greatly to fill in the blanks of this forgotten or neglected history.

It should be noted, however, that this volume is not intended merely as an historical document, nor is its purpose to provoke what Alexander calls "authentic horror for innocent contemporary readers of memoir prose." Its main purpose should be to inspire younger anarchists and those just entering our movement. With over 70 years as an anarchist, Alexander's longevity and unswerving commitment to our movement is impeccable. But we should remember, he has never been alone in his level of commitment. He and countless other anarchists endured years of prison, concentration camps and exile, as well as being constantly watched and monitored by police spies and informers. They responded with incredible acts of courage and expressions of solidarity. Alexander and his comrades refused to give up, thus keeping the anarchist flame burning throughout the Stalinist years, and paving the way for a new generation of anarchists in Bulgaria.

It is this which should be an inspiration and shining example to us all.

Rob Blow, October 2013

NOTE ON THE TEXT

The reader will notice in the text, what appear to be occasional irregularities in the capitalization of certain terms. At times, the word 'Communist' is used, and at other times, 'communist'. This is simple differentiation. The term communist, written as lower case, is someone who believes in communism, a doctrine which takes many forms: state, libertarian, council, anarchist, etc. Communist or Communism written with a capital 'C', on the other hand, refers only to the orthodox Marxist-Leninist or Bolshevik varieties, in the case of this book, the Stalinists of the Bulgarian Communist Party or the Communist Party of the Soviet Union. In addition, while the term 'agrarian' may refer to a farmer, peasant or agricultural labourer, readers will also note the frequent use of the capitalized word 'Agrarian' to denote members of the political party known as the Bulgarian Agrarian National Union (BANU).

When transposing Bulgarian and other Slavic words and names from Cyrillic to Latin script, the translator and I have aimed to make the text as accessible as possible for the English speaking reader. Thus, the English letter 'y' is preferred to the letter 'j' in names; thus 'Boyan', instead of 'Bojan'. In this way, the English speaking reader will be more likely to read names with at least a certain degree of accuracy. There are, however, a couple of exceptions to this rule in cases where there is an already established English usage, for example, with the Polish military leader and Bolshevik politician, General Jaruzelski, and the Macedonian city of Skopje.

RB

OFFICIAL DOCUMENT FROM THE ARCHIVES OF BULGARIAN STATE SECURITY*

A. M. Nakov, Anarchist Militant.

The document printed below was lifted from the records of the Prefecture of Police in Pernik, Bulgaria and it concerns an anarchist militant by the name of Alexander Metodiev Nakov. It was passed to us by the Bulgarian Libertarian Union (ULB) in exile whose accompanying note stresses that "this anarchist's dossier is a splendid biography supplied by the police themselves" and adds: "For this testimonial, Nakov is indebted and we are all grateful to the DS (Security Directorate) and its agents, the informants whose names are given inside inverted commas. It is more than just a simple biography of an anarchist fighting for freedom and justice: it amounts to a multi-biography of an entire people in its unflinching struggle."

We have decided to retain the essential style and pattern of the text, contenting ourselves with eliminating the biographical details of A. M. Nakov's two brothers and two sisters.

**Confidential State Security Files
Top Secret Document, Sole Copy
Report on Alexander Metodiev Nakov**

Alexander Metodiev Nakov was born on 1st August 1919 in the village of Kosacha, Pernik department, a Bulgarian, resident in the town of Pernik at No 86, Machala Teva, in the 'Petko Napetov' district. Works in the 'Republic' mine as a locomotive fitter.

*Editorial Note: this document and the accompanying notes were originally published in **Nash Pŭt** (Our Way), organ of the Paris-based ULB. A French translation was subsequently published in **L'Arc**, Revest-Saint-Martin, No. 91/92, 1984, pp. 148-151.

Educated to 7th grade. Descended from a
poor family. Married: two children. His
wife, Kirilka Alexeyeva Metodieva, born 28th
September 1922, in the village of Viskar,
Pernik department, lives at No 86, Machala
'Teva' and works at the 'Machinostroitel'
plant in Pernik as a factory hand. As
in the past, she is today non-party
(apolitical): under her husband's influence,
her position towards the popular authorities
is unfriendly.

His daughter Yordanka Alexeyeva Nakov, born
8th September 1945, in Pernik, is a student,
a member of the DKMS [Dimitrov Communist
Youth League, *ed.*].

His son, Marin Alexandrov Nakov, born March
1948, in Pernik, is a student, a member of
the DKMS.

His father, Metodi Nakov, is long
since deceased.

His mother, Yordanka Christova Nakova, was
born on 2nd July 1897, in Kosacha village,
Pernik department, and resides in the same
village as an apolitical housewife.
The subject in question has two brothers and
two sisters.

Alexander Metodiev Nakov, following his
primary schooling, worked for a time as
a farmhand: after arriving in Pernik,
he started work in the mines in Pernik.

At present he works as a fitter in the 'Republic' mine. *As a worker and producer, he is very good and carries out his production tasks conscientiously.*

As early as 1937, he entered the ranks of the anarchist movement and embarked upon militant activity: he helped launch an anarchist group among the workers of the erstwhile machine department of what is now the 'Machinostroitel' plant.

In 1941, the subject and five other anarchists were arrested by the police and sentenced to 6-8 years in close custody. He served 3 years in prison. After release from prison, he stayed in his native village, carrying on with his anarchist activity along with the subjects Milcho Slavov, Asparoukh Grouzhov, Yordan Borisov, and Gueorgui Kirilov, all of them from Kosacha village. At the end of 1944, he came to Pernik to work: and took up with Dimitri Vassiliev, Boyan Alexev, Laserman Asenov Minev, Maria Duganova, Kotze Zacharinov and others. They set up an 'Élisée Reclus' anarchist organization. The subject was Southwest Bulgarian Anarchist Union's organizing officer for the town of Stanke Dimitrov. After the anarchist movement was outlawed, the subject carried on with his activity as a militant, taking part in an illegal anarchist conference, distributing mutual aid stamps and collecting funds for anarchists hit by reprisals. As a result

of this activity he was sent in 1948 to
the Belene Labour and Re-education Camp,
where he behaved very badly, being punished
several times as a result. He was freed
from the camp on 10th August 1953.

After his release from the camp, he
carried on with his anarchist activity and
frequenting anarchist circles. His closest
connections are Dimitri Vassiliev Stoyanov,
with whom he shared lodgings for a time;
Boyan Alexev Stefanov; Mikhail Stoyanov
Mindov, presently at No 2, 'Batak' Street in
Ruse, Vladimir Andonov and Iliya Gueorguiev
Minev. At present the subject meets
frequently with the above-named anarchists;
they discuss events, swap literature and
assist one another.

In the labour and re-education camp, the
subject met lots of anarchists from all
parts of the country, with whom he remains
in ongoing contact. In August 1961, using
his warrant for free nationwide rail travel,
he travelled to Varna, there to meet with
Boyan Todorov Mangov, Atanase Mangov and
Todor Baramov, very active anarchists: in
Kolarovgrad he met with Troufcho Nikolov
Troufchev: in Knegea, with Trifon Todorov
Tersijski: in Debeletz, with Lecho Todorov
Nachev: and in Sandanski, with Petko lvanov
Stoyanov: he discussed their connections and
morale with them all.

The subject's attitude towards the popular

authorities is unfriendly: he makes scurrilous comments, damaging the prestige of the popular authorities.
Concerning the change in the currency, and in the presence of agent 'Nikolov', he made a remark to the effect that in the wake of the change the price of goods would be increasing and the workers' wages shrinking.

Apropos of the 25th February 1962 elections, the subject made a statement that the elections are not free, but rather a consequence of the Communists' disarray.

In the presence of agent 'Bogdanov', he declared: "Scrutinize events through the prism of a free-thinker who cannot swallow the dogmas of the present communists and then you will understand and see where the world is headed. The Communists have stripped peoples of all power and provoked their resistance throughout Eastern Europe, especially in Poland, Hungary and East Germany. There the authorities only manage to hang on thanks to Russian pikes. The Hungarian events are a good example and confirmation of that."

In character, the subject is modest, a teetotaller, a non-smoker and a fine worker. He is possessed of a good overall political grounding, reads a lot, knows Esperanto and is a member of the New Path Esperantist society in Pernik. He is a fanatical anarchist who openly declares that nothing

on earth can divorce him from his ideas and
from his relations with anarchists.

The subject was taken to the OND No 1218
from 1954 to February 1962.

Mobilization papers.
Drafted by: P. Videnov
Approved.
Chief of Mobilization Service
Assistant Colonel - [*illegible*]
Service Seal

Note from the Bulgarian Libertarian Union in exile

The above text is a translation from an original authen-
ticated by the Bulgarian Libertarian Union in exile as a photo-
copy of the original, sole existing document registered by the
MVR [Ministry of Interior] Prefecture in Pernik. Comment
would be pointless. But there are a few necessary points that
we ought to make clear:

1. As a document, its status is that of a HISTORICAL CER-
    TIFICATE prepared by the regime of 'People's Democracy'
    for its own use, which is to say by and for the Bulgarian
    CP as the vanguard of the working class, governing in the
    name of the class and targeting with its 'dictatorship of the
    proletariat', not merely the 'enemy', but the most typical
    representatives of the world of work.

2. The document shows how painstakingly the police prepare
    their files on enemies of the working class's very own re-
    gime, because the intelligence collected relates not only to
    the 'enemy' himself but also to his wife, children, brothers
    and sisters, and not even his mother and his dead father
    are overlooked.

3. The 'subject' who is not a human being but merely No 1218 on a police register is, in this instance, an anarchist, a member of the anarchist movement from the age of 18, having served jail time for his beliefs and his militant activities under the old regime and been interned under the current one for years even after the compilation of this file, in 1978, for collecting mutual aid stamps and having helped those of his comrades suffering under 'reprisals', according to the document itself, and who are many, being a 'great' many from 'all around the country'.

4. This anarchist's file is a magnificent biography (drawn up by the police themselves) of what can be achieved, one which should be a source of pride not only to the worldwide anarchist movement, but above all also to the working class, which has in him an outstanding representative.

5. This anarchist, an enemy of the regime, "product of a very poor village family and not of the bourgeoisie" is a worker, who "as a worker and producer, is very good and he carries out his production tasks conscientiously," and is neither a saboteur, slacker, hooligan, nor mollycoddled bum. "By nature he is modest and industrious, and doesn't drink or smoke." Nakov is grateful for this testimonial and we are all in the debt of the DS (Security Directorate) and its agents, the informers whose names are given in inverted commas. It is not merely a biography of an anarchist fighting for freedom and justice, but a genuine multi-biography of an entire people in its unflinching resistance.

— *The Bulgarian Libertarian Union in exile*

Note by the representative of the FACB (Bulgarian Anarchist Communist Federation) in exile:

"At one time or another I have worked in concert with every one of the comrades named in this article, with the exception of Alexander Nakov's family."

Thanks to Paul Sharkey for the translation of the above, and to the Kate Sharpley Library for their kind permission, allowing us to use the above text.

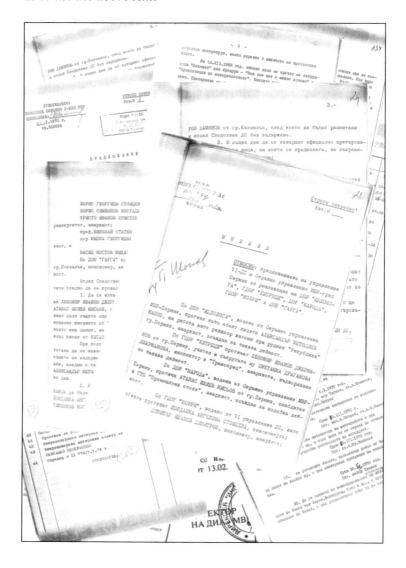

CHAPTER 1: AUTOBIOGRAPHY of ALEXANDER NAKOV

Why did I become an anarchist, a *bezvlastnik*? I deliberately repeat the word in the exact Bulgarian[*] because, in the brainwashed minds of many, anarchy means lack of order, chaos and destruction. In fact, its meaning is "non-power" or "no to power": no to power as an instrument of oppression, no to exploitation, no to irresponsible government over obedient human masses, no to any kind of power exercised by one human over another.

Why did I remain a committed anarchist for over 70 years? Yes, it has been 70 years. My anarchist path began before I was 17, in that distant year of 1936, the year of the Spanish Revolution, in which the anarchists were its soul. For me and for many of my peers, the reasons were the excitement of youth, revolutionary romanticism and the impulse towards giving and receiving support and solidarity. Later, I came to understand more and more. I read widely and was interested in what the other political schools of thought offered on the social question. I voraciously followed events at home and abroad. And the more I read and observed, the stronger my conviction in the anarchist idea grew. No other political doctrine, no party offered true freedom and social justice. Hitlerism and Bolshevism, which had initially claimed to be defending the working masses, proved to be the greatest tyrants to have violated working people and the free spirit of humanity in general.

This is the foundation upon which I built my convictions and my life.

I was born into a miserably poor peasant family on August 1 1919, in the village of Kosacha near Pernik. My father died in 1929 when I was a ten-year-old second-grade student in the

---

[*] The author uses both the word anarchist and the purely Bulgarian word *bezvlastnik* (literally, without a ruler) in the original.

Basin and Seams of the "Pernik" Mine

village elementary school. I had two brothers and two sisters, all of whom were younger than me. My grandfather, Nako, was 96 years old. My mother was sickly, burdened with caring for us youngsters, so I had to leave school and work to earn as much as I could.

I took up jobs at small groceries and pubs in Sofia and Pernik. Everything I earned, I gave to my mother. It was just enough to provide bread for the family.

In December 1934, I took a job at a food stall in front of the Tsaleva Krusha Coal Mine in Pernik. The man who was renting the stall, 'Uncle' Yordan, and his wife, 'Auntie' Milka[*], had three children and maintained quite a modest living. I felt like an extra burden on this family so, after a month, I left. I sought a new, possibly better paid job. So in February 1935 I started with Atanas Nakov, who at the time was a lime trader and producer in Pernik. My job was at the lime-pit near the Kristal glass factory. For a lad like me, the work was

---

[*] The terms 'Uncle' and 'Auntie' are not used to indicate blood relatives but as a sign of respect or familiarity.

heavy. The working day lasted 12 hours. In the summer,
the heat from the sun and the
ovens was unbearable. But I
had no choice. I had to work
even though I had become
as thin as a rake. My mother, my sisters and brothers
relied solely on my wages to
survive.

In the autumn of the same
year, 1935, the boss opened
up a new enterprise, a store-
house for grains, flour and
bran. I became a "trade em-
ployee" – a shop assistant in
the store. I was just 16 years
old. My new job allowed me
more spare time to socialize
with people my own age and
to commute to my village on Sundays. Our neighbourhood,
Pueva Mahala, was a remote neighbourhood, situated four
kilometres from the village centre. Depending on the season,
I would contribute to the agricultural work. I learned how
to mow, plough, sow and so on – everything related to the
village economy.

Sofia, 1933. Liuben (waiter, on the left),
Stoyan Bivolorov (chef's assistant) and
Alexander Nakov (buffet attender, in the
middle) at a restaurant in Sofia.

In 1936 I had already met and befriended some young
anarchists in Pernik. The revolution in Spain began in the
same year, with anarchists acting as its driving force. One
youth, Milen Pavlov, supplied me with a newsletter printed illegally by the Federation of Anarchist Communists in
Bulgaria (FACB). This newsletter presented events in Spain
quite differently to what could be read in the Bulgarian press.
The Bulgarian press was censored and could hardly be called
independent. A much more suitable description would be

"sell-out" or "yellow" press.

At that time, there was a notable group of anarchists in my village, Kosacha. Of these, the older members were Asen Tomov, a lawyer, Peter Dimitrov, a teacher, and Metodi Dimitrov, a mine engineer. The younger ones were Liubenov, Yordan Tomov, Bogdan Tsvetkov, Bogdan Aleksov, Stamen Dimitrov, Liuben Gospodinov Liubenov, the brothers Yordab and Hristo Pavlovi, the brothers Yordan and Stefan Georgiev, George Yordanov Bozhilov, Milcho Krumov and George Kirilov. The whole of Kosacha's youth gravitated around them.

No young people in Kosacha chose to join the youth organizations of either the Communists or the Agrarians*. All cultural events were organized by the anarchists, despite the fact that everything was publicized as the work of the House of Culture (*chitalishte*),† which incidentally had a very rich library. Following Kimon Georgiev's coup in 1934‡, all "dangerous literature" was banned and confiscated from the library. However, 'Uncle' Pesho (this was what we called the teacher, Peter Dimitrov), who was also a librarian, cannily managed to hide almost all of the books with anarchist content and was later able to lend these out for reading. The second purge was carried out by the Bolsheviks after 9ᵗʰ September 1944 but 'Uncle' Pesho once again saved a number of items.

In Pernik, anarchist literature was supplied by our tireless comrade, Laserman Asenov Minev, who worked as a turner at the machine unit of the Mini Pernik mine. The young people involved in anarchist propaganda included Milen Pavlov, Boyan Aleksov, Ivan Pavlov, Todor Kirov Zlatkov, Boris Iv.

* Members of the Bulgarian Agrarian National Union (BANU), a peasant organization.

† A *chitalishte* (literally, "reading room") is a public institution and building which fulfills several functions at once, such as a community centre, library, and a theatre.

‡ One of the leaders of the right wing military Zveno movement, influenced by the fascist corporatism of Mussolini. Georgiev was later involved with the Bulgarian Communist Party.

Anarchist youth of Pernik.

Serginov, his brother Vasil and his sister Vera, Boris Tsvetkov and Metodi Yanev. Of the older ones, I remember Dimiter Vasilev Achanov, Boyan 'The Granny' Aleksandrov, Yordan Kolev (the teacher), Boris Markovenski, George Panayotov, Yordan Georgiev and Bozhichko Hristov.

At that time, many anarchists from the villages were students at the high school in Pernik but I had little contact with them, even though I knew many anarchist students there. There were students from Zemen, Trekliano and elsewhere. In Pernik we were hiding an illegal comrade from Ruse, whose real name was Kiril Kunev Arnaudov – his underground name was Kiril Gaberov. We acquired a duplicator* and almost every night at Kiril's place, we printed leaflets, newssheets, appeals and manifestos on it. Our propaganda against the "brown plague" that was sweeping across Europe was of a high quality. At the time, our most frequent and enthusiastic propaganda leaflets were those in support of the Spanish Revolution.

---

* Also known as a stencil duplicator or mimeograph, a machine for printing propaganda relatively inexpensively.

CHAPTER 2: ESPERANTO

It was toward the end of 1936. I was walking along Pernik's main street and, as usual, I stopped to look in the window of the Vuglen Bookshop.* Among the books on display lay an Esperanto textbook. I already knew that it was an international language, created precisely to ease communication between people of different countries. This appealed to me. Besides, I had heard it was easy to learn. Esperanto bulletins covering events in Spain were available in Bulgaria and I wanted to be able to read them for myself. I went in and bought the book, which had been written by Ivan Krustanov. The book was richly illustrated but I did not know any of the Latin letters, so I had to start by learning the alphabet. I was not good at grammar, even in Bulgarian, so it was difficult from the outset. However, my persistence knew no bounds, although, when I got to the accusative case, I was almost ready to abandon the book.

One evening, on New Year's Eve 1937, I stopped by the "Teetotaller" pastry shop to treat myself to a mug of *boza*†. The pastry shop was situated in the market square across from what was then the market hall. A young man there was just offering the owner an Esperanto calendar for 1937. I was speechless with joy. I introduced myself to the young man. His name was Boris Serginov and he worked as a mechanic. I started speaking to him in Esperanto but soon switched to Bulgarian. I explained to him how far I had got with the language but that I could not cope with the accusative case. He encouraged me and promised to call for me at my workplace to help me out. So that was how it happened. After he explained it several times, the problem was gone. In the meantime, I met a barber, Stoyan Milanov Kirov, who like me had been studying Esperanto alone. Whenever we met, usually

---

* This translates as the Charcoal Bookshop.

† A low alcohol, below 1%, fermented malt drink.

Boris Vasev and Alexander Nakov, 1937

on the station platform, we made an effort to speak only in Esperanto. Even though this was difficult at the beginning, it gradually got easier. I met other Esperantists, too, such as Vasil Velchev, Kosta Hadzhiev, and Geo Vuzharov, Georgi Idakiev and his wife, who had mastered the language better than any of us. At a meeting of young anarchists on Vitosha Mountain*, I met Anka Pisarska, who studied at the midwifery school on Cyrill and Methodius Street in Sofia. Later she married the anarchist, Boris Menkov, took his name and went to live with him in Kiustendil. That is why I mention her as Anka Menkova from here on. Anka greatly helped me to master Esperanto grammar. So again, as well as my own personal persistence, the help of my comrades was crucial. There were no private lessons and no paid classes. We were poor, inspired, and dedicated.

Not long after, I was able to read, speak, and write properly. I started to correspond with Esperantists from within the country and abroad. We established an Esperanto society in Pernik, called "New Path" (*Nova Vojo*). Some of the members were experienced Esperantists such as Anton Vasev and

---

* A popular place for hiking, near to Sofia.

Nikola Mitev, while others were beginners. Esperanto classes were set up for adults and school students, and organizational and educational meetings were held. Many young people, such as Tsvetana Popova, Tsvetana Zareva, Maritsa Popova, Pera Ivanova, Snezhana Zhoteva, Raina Agontseva, Georgi Hristov, and Velin Takev learned the language well. Members attended international Esperanto congresses. I, however, was not allowed to leave the country. I attended all the congresses held in Bulgaria, apart from when I was in Bolshevik camps and in exile. While I was locked up in the fascist prisons (1941-1944), I was in contact with good Esperantists like Asen Grigorov, the author of Esperanto books and dictionaries, as well as with other comrades. In the concentration camps, too, I found people to converse with in Esperanto such as Gancho Lazarov Damianov, and we missed no opportunity to speak in our favourite language.

I subscribed to many Esperanto journals published in this country and abroad. The Bulgarian journals were *Bulgara Esperantisto* and *Nuntempa Bulgario* (a journal exclusively for external propaganda). The foreign ones were *Heroldo de Esperanto*, *Esperanto*, *El Popola Ĉinio*, *Sennaciulo*, *Norda Prismo* and *Liberecana Ligilo*, the latter being illegal in Bulgaria*. Unfortunately, along with all of my correspondence, my Esperanto publications were confiscated twice from my home; once on 16th December 1948 and a second time in March 1974.

In more recent times, this wonderful language has been losing followers in Bulgaria. Fewer and fewer people attend congresses each year.

Incidentally, on several occasions, the Bulgarian Esperanto Association has acknowledged me with various awards for promoting the language. I remain Treasurer of the Pernik Esperanto Society to this day.

---

* *Liberecana Ligilo* is an anarchist publication.

CHAPTER 3: 1938 – 1942

In 1938, after a short preparation, I passed my exam for the seventh grade. In 1939, the Spanish Revolution was crushed by world capitalism led by German Nazism and Italian fascism, but also, not without the contemptible assistance of Bolshevik Russia. In March, the last revolutionaries withdrew from Spain. There were many Bulgarian anarchists among them. The best known among these was Todor Angelov Bozhanata, who subsequently organized resistance against the German occupation of Belgium and became a national hero of that county – but not a hero in Bulgaria! Later the Bolsheviks tried to posthumously appropriate his name and his glory, the way they did with others who fought fascism, such as poets and thinkers. But their efforts were useless. The world knew. There followed the signing of the long in preparation pact between Bolshevik Russia and Nazi Germany, known as the Ribbentrop-Molotov Pact of 23rd August 1939. After the signing of this disgraceful pact, we, the Bulgarian anarchists, now as the only organized antifascists in the country, had to conduct propaganda alone against the brown plague. The Communists, obeying their proverbial party discipline, kept silent. So, the monarch's police persecuted only us.

At this time, there were three anarchist organizations in Pernik: the Federation of Anarchist Youth (FAM), of which I was a member; an ideological organization with an adult membership[*]; and the syndicalist organization, which, following Laserman Asenov Minev's suggestion, was named the Workers Defence Organization (ZRO). The latter organization had a larger membership because its membership contained not only convinced anarchists but also anarchist sympathisers. This organization was established in 1937 and it existed almost up to the end of the war. After the Bolshevik coup on 9th September 1944, it did not resume activities. De-

---

[*] This would presumably be the FACB.

spite its larger membership, the ZRO was never discovered by the police, even though some of its members were locked up in the prisons and concentration camps.

By 1940, I was already a soldier in the army of the monarchy. I served in the town of Dupnitsa in the 4th Anti-Aircraft Battery. As head of a family, I served a reduced term. While there, I used my leave time to meet with anarchist comrades from Dupnitsa for several hours at a time. The prominent anarchists there were Vlado Kitnov, Pantelei Popdimitrov, Hristo 'The Rabbit' Manolov and others living in the town at the time. After my discharge at the beginning of October, I returned to work in the town of Pernik and was back with my anarchist comrades. Once again, I was operating the duplicator, putting newssheets together, midnight meetings, linking up with comrades from the villages around the towns of Pernik, Radomir, Dupnitsa, and Kiustendil, meeting up with new comrades, distributing literature, and writing and disseminating leaflets on numerous occasions, most frequently in relation to the already raging World War II.

On the 19th of January 1941, I brought my mother a daughter-in-law from Pernik. In early February, Kirilka Aleksova Stefanova, the sister of my good comrade Boyan Aleksov Stefanov, and I got married. On February 20th, I was conscripted in Sofia, into the 4th Artillery Regiment. On the day I donned my military clothes, the chief of State Security (known as the DS) in Pernik, named Kisyov, arrived at the barracks. He demanded that the commander of the unit transfer me to the investigating authorities of State Security. However, the commander refused, stating that the corresponding investigation could be conducted at the barracks. I found out from Kisyov that anarchists had been arrested in Pernik on charges of conspiracy. I was supposed to be charged with the same. I was expected to admit to my participation in this conspiracy, which had already been confirmed by some of those arrested. However, I denied involvement, only admitting to giving books to two of the accused. With that, the "investigation" at the barracks was over. But after my demobilization in July 1941, I was handed over to the police and, as a person under investigation, was taken to the disciplinary prison in Kiustendil.

Upon arrival, I was thrown into a large cell, full of young anarchists from the villages around Dupnitsa. All of them were under 20 years of age. I was the eldest at 21. We passed the time until sunset getting to know one another. We had interesting conversations, mostly about the new war between

With Kirilka, 1938, somewhere between the villages Vrania stena, Zemen and Peshtera in the Radomir area

the former allies, Nazi Germany and Soviet Russia. Everyone was hoping that the Bolsheviks would now turn antifascist again. I remember the names of a few of these boys: Naiden Elenin, Slavcho Boshov, Ivan Drundov, Boris Markov, Vidin Shalvarkov. I think there were eight of them. One other, Alexander Dimitrov, was kept in solitary confinement in a separate, small cell.

When the evening checks began, the warders singled out one of the youths to read the evening prayer. He refused. Then they pointed at me. "Well then, let's have the new one read it!" I refused. Then they said they would put me in solitary. But as soon as they reached for me, Vidin Shalvarkov took off his sandal and stood between me and the warder, with a sandal in his hand, raised and ready to strike. The other boys brandished their sandals too. The three screws backed off and hurried out. That evening, they left us alone. On the following day, all the boys' relatives came from Dupnitsa for a visit. So while I was alone in the cell, the screws came in and took me away. I ended up in solitary, where I spent all of the remaining few days before I was transferred from that prison.

Boyan Aleksov

In the period 1945-1948, Vidin Shalvarkov and I bumped into each other more than once in relation to the various organizational needs of the movement. Later, we came to spend a longer time together in the concentration camps; first at Bogdanov Dol, then at Belene. Vidin stoically endured the inhuman conditions, remaining true to his ideals and was a selfless comrade. After we were released from camp, we continued to meet to exchange news, thoughts, and the scarce literature that was left here and there, in attics and basements. After 10th November 1989, when an opportunity emerged for the Bulgarian Anarchist Federation (FAB) to act more or less legally, Vidin and other comrades from Dupnitsa re-established the organization there. Vidin tirelessly established connections with the comrades from the surrounding villages. His severe and prolonged illness did not crush his belief in the ideal he had lived with. He died on 20th August 2001, two months after his 80th birthday.

From the prison in Kiustendil, I was transferred to Sofia's Central Prison. Locked up there, were the comrades from my trial – Boyan Aleksov Stefanov, Vladimir Petrov, Boris Tsvetkov, and Simeon Yanev. Kiril Kunev Arnaudov had managed to hide. We were tried under Article II of the notorious Defence of the State Act (ZZD). I received a term of ten years in prison, but because I was still considered a minor by the laws of the time, they reduced the sentence to six years and eight months, plus a fine of 50,000 lev.

Kiril Arnaudov received the harshest sentence. He was not lucky enough to taste prison life but instead opted for a life of illegality. When hiding in different towns became too risky and even impossible, he and Ivan Mangurov took to the mountains. However, a few days before 9th September, they were liquidated, not by the fascists but by the Bolsheviks, somewhere in the Rhodopi Mountains.

In addition to the comrades from my trial, I ran into four Bolsheviks in the Central Prison. These were Asen Grigorov, a good Esperantist, Vlado Georgiev, Subi Enev, and a younger man whose name I have forgotten. They were doing time related to older sentences. Later I found out that the Bolsheviks raised a monument to Vlado Georgiev in Samokov.

The Agrarians constituted the largest group of political prisoners. There were three persons sentenced to death in the Gemeto trial*. I remember there being 47 Agrarians there. Initially there were three prisoners per cell, but when the Bolsheviks were attacked by their "ally", they became anti-fascist, and so the monarchists began to persecute and arrest them. Around the end of 1941 and the beginning of 1942, mass arrests of Bolsheviks were under way and the cells in the Central Prison were not able to hold us all. Between 10 and 12 men were locked in cells built to fit three.

In the meantime, a new anarchist group had been uncovered in southwest Bulgaria. The following comrades were arrested: Dimitur Vasilev from Pernik; Milcho Slavov Liubenov from Kosacha village; Viktor Popdimitrov Rizov, a student from Perivol village; Petur 'The Camel', a graduate in medicine; Peiko Raikov Ganchev, a chemist and technician; Borislav Menkov, a student from Kiustendil; Stanimir Kotev, a forester; Vasil 'The People' Todorov; and others. We had endless arguments with the Bolsheviks on all kinds of topics. There was a large group of young Jewish boys who were interested in learning about the ideals of anarchism. But the

* Gemeto was George Mihov Dimitrov, leader of the BANU.

famous future Bolshevik leader, who was a Komsomol member at the time, Zhivko Zhivkov[*], dispersed them every time he saw them hanging out with us. This continued in Skopje Prison, but there he chased them away with a stick! In order to end the arguments with some kind of mutual understanding, the people from their Central Committee intervened. The cleverest and most patient among them were Traicho Kostov and 'The Mosquito'. Of the Agrarians, I remember Tsenko Barev and Georgi Halachev, a poet with very positive feelings towards anarchism and the anarchists. He was completely blind. I also knew those who were sentenced to death: Sergi Zlatanov, Slavi Popignatov, and another Agrarian whose name I cannot remember.

When I was put in prison, my mother, brothers and sisters, and my wife, too, were left with virtually no material support. My brother Ivan, already a grown-up boy, managed to get a job in Pernik and began to take care of our younger brother, sisters, and mother. My wife relied on her parents' support.

Throughout my time spent in the Central Prison, my wife visited regularly, bringing food and everything I needed. Every other week, my mother would come to visit, and so would my brother Ivan. Due to rationing, they had a tough time obtaining goods for themselves, yet they still brought something for me in prison as well. Comrades not in prison also expressed solidarity. Prison food got worse every month. Our bread allocation was 300 grams per day, while twice a week we received boiled potatoes; three potatoes per person (and every time, at least one of them was inedible). Thanks to the food arriving from outside, and thanks to the mutual aid existing between us, we did not starve.

A piece of paper was attached to the door of the cell. I still remember what it said. The prisoner is entitled to receive food from outside twice a week. Once a week he is entitled to a visit. He has the right to send one letter and to receive

---

[*] A future Politbureau member.

one letter per week. Wake-up time and walks in the prison corridors are regulated, as are the two walks in the prison yard, one in the morning and one in the afternoon. The prisoner has no right to read newspapers or books that are not approved by the prison management. Furthermore, he has to remain silent and stay away from the windows. I may have left out something.

In spite of the strict prohibitions, we managed to procure newspapers from the non-political prisoners. Also, there were two warders from my village who did a few favours for me. Their names were Boris Dimitrov and Ivan Ananiev Gruyov.

When some paratroopers were shot, the Central Committee of the Bolsheviks called a three-day prison hunger strike. Here is how the Bolshevik hunger strike worked. All of us political prisoners returned the food we had received from the prison. But the gentlemen from the Central Committee neither threw away nor shared the food they had stored away in their large suitcases. So only some actually went hungry during those three days.

In the winter of 1941-42, newly uncovered Bolshevik groups were brought into the prison en masse. I realized that Pavel Shatev, known for being one of the Boatmen of Thessaloniki*, had been brought in with one of these groups. I first saw him in the corridor of the Eighth Section when one of the prisoners pointed him out to me. I approached him and introduced myself. When I told him I was an anarchist, tried with other anarchists on charges of conspiracy, he became visibly interested. I did, however, state my surprise at seeing him among the Bolsheviks. He started to beat about the bush, saying that in the struggle, this was not of great significance since fascism oppressed everyone equally. He had joined because he could not bear to remain idle. "That's right," I said, "but each of us has to fight from his own position." After this first conversation, we held many more. I asked him

---

* The Boatmen of Thessaloniki were a turn-of-the-century "propaganda by the deed" group, opposed to Ottoman rule.

about his participation in the assassinations in Thessaloniki and whether all of the participants had been anarchists. He said, yes, there had been no others. He gave me two books in which he had written about his participation in those events, **The Assassins of Salonika** and **An Exile in Fesan**. Years later these books were republished under the single title, **In Macedonia Under the Yoke**. As I understand it, after the fall of the fascist regime, I heard that Pavel Shatev had been included in the new Macedonian government of Apostolski.*

---

* Shatev, 1882-1951, was involved in the formation of the People's Republic of Macedonia and was elected Minister of Justice in the first Bolshevik government there. He was later purged from the Party and jailed for allegedly being pro-Bulgarian and anti-Yugoslav. Eventually placed under house arrest in Bitola, he died in mysterious circumstances – his body was found on Bitola's dung heap in January 1951. Mikhail Apostolski, 1906-1987, was a partisan in the Macedonian National Liberation Army. After the war, he became a military leader in the Socialist Federal Republic of Yugoslavia.

CHAPTER 4: IN THE SKOPJE PRISON

In early March 1943, when the Central Prison became overcrowded, about 400 of us prisoners were loaded onto cattle-trucks at the Central Railway Station in Sofia and taken away. We tried to guess where we were being taken from what we could see through the cracks in our box. In the evening, we ended up at the station at Skopje. Once we had all descended, we were counted to check that no one had escaped. Next, a troop of police took charge of us. We were driven to the Skopje prison. This prison, built under Ottoman rule, had thick walls possibly more than two meters thick, with embrasure-like windows for machine-gun emplacements. Having spent the night with none of us able to sleep, we were taken out into the yard along with the baggage we were carrying. Again, a police troop came and took us away.

After a long trek of about five hours, we found ourselves in the vicinity of Idrizovo village. There, far from the village itself, in the fields near the Thessaloniki-Skopje Road and the Vardar River, we saw a solitary building surrounded by high walls. This was to be our prison. It was a two-story building and there were four dormitories on both the first and second floors. These dormitories were quite spacious. They were furnished inside with two-tier plank-beds, similar to the bunk-beds in holiday chalets. The capacity of each dormitory was 50 people, so all 400 of us were placed in the eight dormitories. There was just one manual water pump in the yard. The cesspit was also in the yard. There was no sewage system. Whenever the pit overfilled, a special vehicle came to pump out the faeces. There was a canteen, too; however, this only sold mouldy carrots and chick peas.

There were seven of us anarchists: Vasil 'The People' Todorov, Dimitur Vasilev, Nikola Mladenov, Pencho Raikov, Milcho Slavov, Boyan Aleksov, and myself. The food we were given was lower than the lowest standard. If you were to drop a coin into a deep food container full of soup, you would probably still be able to see it at the bottom. The bread was made of corn mash and when it was handed out fresh, it was edible, but overnight it turned to stone. And if you kept it even longer, it went mouldy in such a way that it would appear stringy when you broke it.

The money we had soon disappeared; spent on chick peas and mouldy carrots. We made numerous attempts to get in touch with our relatives, but this was in vain. The letters we wrote were most likely destroyed. One day, after nearly a month of starvation and isolation, our comrade Dimitur Vasilev saw a prison guard whom he recognized as someone from his wife's village. He succeeded in convincing him to take a letter and to hand it to his wife in person. The letter contained the addresses of all the anarchists in Skopje Prison. Soon after this, we began to receive parcels. Milcho Slavov's brother-in-law used to work for Skopje's postal service, and he was the first to visit with several suitcases of food. It then turned out that an agronomist from Radomir was employed in Skopje Prison. He also visited us with an impressive amount of food. My brother and my wife visited me, too. They witnessed the bombing in Sofia when they were at the train station. During the visit, which lasted no more than ten minutes, I could tell that my wife was very upset. From Skopje to the prison, they had been given a ride in the official carriage of the same comrade agronomist, Yancho Dobridolski. Food parcels continued to arrive. Each prisoner was entitled to receive one parcel per month, as long as there was someone to send it. And because here we were, now part of "Great Bulgaria", it meant that the Bulgarian police, the Bulgarian army, and the Bulgarian bureaucrats were in charge; the whole administration was Bulgarian*. The war was becoming increasingly more tangible. The Germans had so far not encountered equivalent

---

* They were in Macedonia.

resistance from any other army, whether by surpassing them in number or (so it was assumed) technology. The Bolsheviks in prison were eating their words. Approximately a hundred of these had already signed declarations stating that they had given up their ideas and would serve "Tsar and Fatherland". They were placed under a lighter regime of detention but were still not released. We called these "The Declarants".

Our arguments with the Bolsheviks continued uninterrupted inside the rooms. There was always some reason for these arguments, whether over May Day, Hristo Botev*, the October Revolution, the Paris Commune, the Spanish Revolution, questions of principle, theoretical and practical matters and what not. The best defender of anarchist principles and the best prepared was Vasil Todorov. Two months into our stay at Skopje, four of our comrades were sent to different prisons around the country. Only three of us remained: Pencho Raikov, Nikola Mladenov, and I.

The prison owned a large estate. There was a cowshed, beehives, and a pigsty. Prior to our arrival, only non-political prisoners were engaged on the estate. Once intensive field work started, we political prisoners who had done a third of our sentence were moved to the farm building assigned to the field workers. The Declarants were accommodated there too, serving, as I already mentioned, under a lighter regime. I remember the first day we were taken out to work in the fields; we were assigned to sow sunflowers. There was a total of 35 of us privileged enough to work outside the prison walls. It was indeed a privilege! After hoeing in the spring varieties it was time to mow the meadows. Those of us who worked received a larger bread ration, too. When we worked in the garden, we would persuade the agronomist to let us have something extra for food. He was a good chap and, without management's knowledge, he let us have tomatoes, peppers or potatoes.

---

* The 19th century Bulgarian poet and revolutionary.

There was a non-political prisoner, 'Old' Pencho, who had been accused of murder when he had been a woodsman (he did not admit to committing this crime). He was in charge of the beehives. One day, I persuaded the agronomist to send me over to him as an assistant. There were about 20 hives in the bee-garden. The pasture was very rich but the agronomist was unable to provide either honeycombs, or new beehives. Yet the bees were multiplying daily because they were not being provided with the conditions to work and develop. 'Old' Pencho and I began weaving wicker hives and soon we had enriched the bee-garden with the kind of primitive devices that even the Abyssinians had stopped using. But they worked.

I took advantage of my free movement in the part of the estate that bordered on an acacia wood. A Turkish man regularly grazed his cows there. I succeeded in persuading him, whenever it was possible for him, to bring me a newspaper that was banned within the prison. The Turk agreed that if I left him 10 lev under a rock, he would leave the paper under the same rock. This arrangement continued for a long time. After reading it, I would give the paper to a young Turkish lad doing time for petty theft. This Turkish boy serviced the pump for emptying the cesspit; the pump entered the prison almost daily. So, in turn, he would deliver the paper to my mate, Pencho Raikov. But once, by a ridiculous accident, the Turkish youth, whose name, as I recall, was Munir, did not hide the paper well enough and got caught. During the interrogation he admitted, "Sasho gave it to me."[*]

"Who were you meant to give it to?"

Munir replied that he had taken it to read himself but had forgotten to leave it and had accidentally brought it inside the prison. I was quickly informed of the incident, so soon came up with a reply for the forthcoming interrogation. The prison governor himself called me in. In answer to the question, "Where did you get the paper?" I said that, while I was

---

[*] Sasho is the diminutive of Alexander.

working in the garden, two soldiers had passed by reading a paper, and I asked if I could have it, so they threw it over.

"And why did you give it to the Turkish boy and who was he supposed to give it to?"

I replied that he saw me reading the paper in the toilet and asked me for it.

"I couldn't refuse because I thought that if I didn't give it to him he might rat on me."

Whatever they believed, I spent a week in solitary.

In August, on the 28th to be exact, we found out that our good Tsar, who had sent us to the "New Lands" of his "Great Kingdom" had died suddenly. It was a joyous occasion for all. Some of the prisoners with shorter sentences were released. My good friend, Nikola Mladenov, whose sentence was almost over, was released, too. I found out later that he went to see my mother and my brothers in my village. He also met my wife. As I was now on my own, the authorities offered to move me into one of the cells with the Declarants. I declined, preferring to stay with the criminal prisoners! By the way, there were some good lads among them. They were mostly serving sentences for black-marketeering, which had taken over all aspects of life during the war. I even made friends with a few of those I worked and shared a cell with.

The war was intensifying. We kept getting news of the growing partisan movement both within the country and in Macedonia. Captured or surrendered partisans began to arrive in prison. There were Macedonians, Serbs, and Albanians among them.

At the beginning of 1944, we were able to get more and more news of the Germans getting bogged down in the Bolshevik mire, of the German defeat near Stalingrad and the Anglo-American successes in Africa. All this encouraged the Bolsheviks in prison and they began to discuss (and were even haggling!) who was going to get what position when their party came to power in Bulgaria. I once had the following conversation while strolling in a yard in which there was a water pump with two spouts. The Communist I was walking with said, "Nakov, do you see this water pump?" "Yes," I replied. "When we come to power, butter will flow from one of the spouts and honey will flow from the other." I responded critically, knowing what kind of honey and what kind of butter the Russian peasants ate after the Bolshevik coup. But there were uninformed people who took his words at face value.

In 1944, life in prison was accompanied by the thought that the war would soon be coming to an end. It was now only a question of time, when, rather than who, would win. The victory had been decided when the US joined the war, even if they had joined rather late.

The monotony of daily life in prison continued. It was a big event when visits and food parcels arrived from outside to break this monotony. There were cheerful moments, too, for instance when Rasim the Gypsy became the focus of attention of the poet, Dobri Zhotev, who made him the hero of a collection of humorous poems*.

Towards the end of August 1944, when the Germans were suffering defeat on all fronts and as German troops were withdrawing from Greece in long columns along the Thessaloniki-Skopje road, a noticeable anxiety could be felt among the prisoners. The prison was located less than 300 metres from this road and the Germans would have no problem exterminating us. We tried to persuade the guards to unlock the doors so that we could go, but they hesitated, even though they had seen their bosses flee, one after the other. Only the Senior Prison Officer and the warders were left. The soldiers were also on guard at the front of the prison gate. Arrangements to remain on the alert were eventually agreed with the Senior Prison Officer, and in the event of imminent danger, he would order the warders to unlock the gates.

In the meantime, the Third Partisan Shock Brigade, which

---

* *Dobri* meaning 'Good' Alexander Zhotev, partisan and poet, 1921-1997.

was commanded by Apostolski*, who later became a minister in the Macedonian government, became interested in us. One night, I think it was August 28, a military unit was seen approaching the prison. The warders opened the gates of the main building and the prisoners left and quickly headed towards the Vardar River. When the partisans (for it was them we had seen) reached the prison, they found it empty. Only one warder had stayed behind. He showed them the direction in which the runaways had headed and the partisans followed in that direction. However, those of us who were locked in the farm building, had still not been released. Only when we began breaking the door did a warder come and open it. I stood at the door to make sure that everyone got out. The non-political inmates knew next to nothing about the arrangements to be released in case of danger. Within a short time, everyone from the four dormitories had got out. Some were barefoot, holding in their hands whatever clothes they had managed to grab in the panic. Only one of the non-political prisoners remained at the door, refusing to come with us. His name was Manio and he was from some village near Pleven. I was unable to persuade him to come along with us. Also, I did not have much time and we had to leave.

When I went out into the farmyard, there was a crowd of about 200 people hesitating about which way to run in the dark. I started to shout out loud, "To the Vardar!" and started running in that direction. By the time I reached the edge of the river, I could see the silhouette of a not-too-large group around me. All my non-political mates were there. I had somehow influenced them and they trusted me. We crossed the river and headed west from the prison in order to cross the Thessaloniki railway. Approaching the railway, we made a plan to walk in single file. Munir, the Turk who came from the nearby villages and was familiar with the area and the road, was to lead us. When we got quite close to the railway, Munir

---
* Mikhail Apostolski, see footnote in previous chapter (p. 16).

came back and said, "There's a soldier over there, 20 paces away." The railway line was guarded. There was no time to hesitate. I went to the head of the line and told the others to follow me. It was dark and the soldier had no way of knowing whether or not we were armed. As soon as he noticed us, he got into position, but that was all. We crossed the railway line, stopping after about a hundred meters on the other side. We found ourselves in a melon field where watermelons awaited us. We were all extremely thirsty as no one had thought to bring a bottle of water.

Having satisfied our thirst with a piece of watermelon, we headed in the direction of the nearby mountain, which we had observed earlier from the prison. We had just begun to walk up the slope, when to the left of us, where the village stood, we heard the loud rattle of machine gun fire, rifles, and hand grenades. This lasted for almost half an hour. When the shooting stopped, there followed an eerie silence. We climbed up the slope and stopped to look around and listen for sounds. To the left, coming from the village, we heard the sound of many people talking. Soon after, the sun began to rise. The noise and clattering sounds increased and, from high up, we were able to make out a long line of people. It was our inmates and the partisans. The end result of this was the coming together of our two groups. Together, we felt strong and free!

CHAPTER 5: WITH THE PARTISANS

W hen the sun had fully risen, we were bombarded with heavy artillery fire from the direction of Skopje. Shells began to fall nearby, to the left and right of us, but none fell on us. We approached the forest and soon hid ourselves from the reach of the artillery. The forest, as in the old days, truly was, and still is, the guardian of rebels.

Making ourselves comfortable, we sat or lay down under the trees. We were told what had happened in the village. There had been a military unit there, but when the partisans and the prisoners approached the village, the soldiers panicked and some of them ran away, with others shot while running. Two of the partisans and one of the prisoners were killed. A large amount of abandoned arms was seized. The partisans released the horses that the military had left behind.

In the meadow where we gathered, the partisan leaders split us up into platoons. Firstly, they set apart those of Macedonian or Serbian descent. The remaining 50 pure Bulgarians were placed in a separate group. Around noon, three planes appeared in the sky above us and started dropping bombs, but all the bombs fell around 300 metres away from us. Some cattle were grazing there and those animals probably paid for our sins. In the evening, we left the forest, and after a long trek we reached a village called Paligrad. We made camp right in the middle of the village square where we intended to sleep. Dinner for ten people was distributed from a mess-tin with some broth. There was nothing but salt in the broth. It was enough to sip two or three spoonfuls and you were done, full. We had just settled ourselves onto the bare ground to rest when, suddenly, the sound of drums, flutes and all kinds of noisy instruments began blaring out. On top of all this, we were attacked by hungry fleas, even more dangerous than the drums.

And so, hungry but free, we gradually began to get used to

our new situation. Sometimes we had better luck when we stayed in a richer Albanian village. The region we were in was not part of Albania but the population there was almost all Albanian with a few exceptions. These villages welcomed us with a better menu, such as chick pea bread, bean soup and sometimes a piece of meat. One night, when we were in the fields, a huge cargo plane dropped parachutes carrying a large amount of ammunition, rifles, food and shoes. We Bulgarians were given some red cloth from the parachutes to make ourselves pioneer scarves. When the partisans carried out actions they would ask if anyone among us had done military service, in order for us to go with them. I often joined these groups. I told my friend Pencho never to volunteer for actions as he had not done military service.

Most of the prisoners were young and had not served in the military. Whenever it was convenient, this guy, whose name I have forgotten, and I taught them how to use a gun. Our group of 50 had been given only two Mannlicher* rifles.

Sometime, around the 5th September, the partisans carried out a big action. Divided up into three large groups, we had to attack Sveti Nikola and Goliamo Selo. I was called to the headquarters and, together with a Serb boy, I was instructed how to get to the village, how to attack it and what to do at the Town Hall and the large farm which was situated near the village. Having received these instructions, we were allocated about 20 partisans and 30 Bulgarian prisoners. The village was about five or six kilometres away. This time, each prisoner was given an Italian rifle and bullets. We set off. While on the road, I decided to check everyone's weapons and discovered that many had bullets from different calibre rifles in their pockets. I made them get rid of all but the Italian bullets. When we reached the village, my first task was to place five or six men on either side of the road. At the first house we reached, we captured the owner, who was just getting ready

---
* Austrian made firearms.

for bed. Initially, he refused to cooperate but we soon convinced him he had no choice but to show us the location of the Town Hall, the farm, and the police station, if there was one. According to HQ's instructions, we sent one group to break into the Town Hall, take anything of value they might find and destroy any archives they found inside. The archive was burned in the Town Hall yard and the cash box was pried open and emptied of its last lev. The group with which we attacked the farm was larger. The guards had abandoned their rifles at their sentry posts and fled. There was a large building in the farm yard and music could be heard coming from one of the rooms. The Serb and I ran in with pointed guns. Five people were having a party inside. We had surprised them. It was obvious they had not been warned. There were glasses of wine and some snacks on the table. An elderly woman was serving the participants of the party. We ordered them to raise their hands. The Serb said, "Does anyone have a gun?" and they all replied that they did not. Our search, however, revealed one gun. When I asked its owner, "Why did you lie?" he told me he did not understand because this was a pistol and not a gun. It turned out that one of the men was a pilot, another was the farm manager, and the rest were his guests. We arrested everyone but the woman. The farm turned out to be very rich. We loaded up sugar, rice, cheese, and other products from the warehouse. When we started taking cases of soap, one of the cow-herds mentioned that the soap was to be distributed to the villagers. Maybe everything else we had taken was also meant to be distributed out. However, we were also in need of food. So, in the end, we finished the job without a single shot as the village was paralysed with no will to resist.

We were to the west of the Vardar River, in a village called Lisiche, when the partisans' radio station, maintained by an English group, announced that, with the aid of the Red Army, the Fatherland Front (Bolshevik) had taken power in Bulgaria.

The Bulgarian Komsomol members were ecstatic. We began to think of returning to Bulgaria.

One day, sometime after 15ᵗʰ September, we were transferred from the Third Macedonian Brigade to the Eighth Serbian Brigade at Bruko. It was soon supposed to be heading across the Vardar to accompany us on some of our journey. One evening, we were told to get ready for the road. We set off and, in order to cross the railway guarded by Germans, we were prepared for battle. But as we were some distance away from this small train station we were approaching, the Germans spotted us and opened up with chaotic machine-gun fire. The partisans and we, the prisoners, took cover in the dark as best as we could. The Germans continued firing at us until the Thessaloniki-Skopje train passed us and we were able to use it as cover to get away. Next, we had to wade into the deep and cold Vardar River. We were freezing cold that morning as our clothes dried on our backs.

Upon arriving at the Pchinya River, we ran into about five thousand Bulgarian army soldiers who had been disarmed by the Germans and were getting ready to return to Bulgaria. Only the officers still had their pistols so there was not much military loot left for us. We collected their pistols and took it upon ourselves to escort them to the Bulgarian border because we were the only ones who were armed. As the army of occupation, let us not forget that the Bulgarian Army had won the "love" of the local population from which we now had to rescue it. When we reached Kratovo we stopped guarding the former soldiers. They had to pass over to the Bulgarian side without our help. It was not far at this point. Several incidents occurred with them on the way to Kratovo. The soldiers had packed their bags so heavily that they could hardly carry them. As soon as a soldier would fall behind or step aside to "rest", several hungry Macedonians would jump out of the bushes and liberate his backpack. Some soldiers were left only in their underwear and if someone tried to resist, he was murdered.

As I mentioned, we were starving more at this time than when we were in prison. So, when we were in Kratovo and saw the ripe figs there, we ate until we were full. From Kratovo we headed towards the border separately. Not far from the border, a regiment of the Bulgarian Army showed up. They were armed with all sorts of weapons: machine-guns, mortars, rifles, sub-machine-guns, and hand grenades. Three Serbian partisans suddenly appeared carrying a piece of paper. They called the Commanding Officer, showed him the paper, and explained that, according to a treaty signed between the Serbian and Bulgarian military, troops not in combat with the Germans were now supposed to be disarmed. Initially, the Commanding Officer refused but a few smart Bolsheviks among us intervened in the Serbs' favour. It was a pathetic sight, watching an army of two-thousand men throw down their arms. Later on, when we were alone and preparing to cross the border, I told one of these know-it-alls that this organized military unit could have been immediately directed by the new Bulgarian government against the Germans. In a typically Bolshevik manner, he replied that a subordinate could not advise his superiors. This self-styled commander's name was Petur and he came from a village near Biala Slatina.

We spent the night near the top of Mount Ruen[*]. By morning, many of us had caught a chill. We descended to the village of Bogoslov near Kiustendil. A partisan unit was billeted in the school there. They welcomed us and gave us half a loaf of bread and a cup of milk each. We spent until sunset familiarizing ourselves with recent events in Bulgaria. The partisans, who were getting ready to cross over to Giueshevo, wanted us to go with them.

None of us volunteered to accompany them. I went to the headquarters and said that these boys still did not know

[*] At 2,251 metres, the highest peak in the Osogovo Mountains in Bulgaria's Kiustendil region.

how to use weapons, that they had not seen their families in years and that they would be much more useful in their home towns. It seemed that my words had an impact. The partisans no longer insisted we went along with them. The following morning, after Pencho and I had finished breakfast, we had to board the train. As I was armed with a Schmeiser* and Pencho had a carbine rifle, several of the partisans surrounded us and made us hand over our weapons. We had no choice. This was the end of our journey together. The guys who, along the way, I had taught to at least make basic use of a rifle, had been quick to report to the partisans that Pencho and I were not Bolsheviks.

---

* A German sub-machine gun.

CHAPTER 6: THE RETURN

Pencho and I went down to Kiustendil, where our comrades greeted us warmly. They gave us food and we discussed the situation in Bulgaria. They were disappointed to hear that the partisans had taken our weapons. I was most heartily welcomed by the anarchist family of Borislav and Anka Menkovi, whom I had been very close to even before I went to prison. I had known Anka, a bright and faithful person, ever since she was a student at the midwifery school in Sofia. At the time, she had helped me greatly with my Esperanto studies. Later she married 'Wild' Borislav, a former member of the International Brigades in Spain, and who was later sent to the concentration camp at Belene. Anka bore him two sons. The Menkovis insisted that we stay the night with them. I told them it would take them a month to get rid of the lice we would infest them with if we were to stay over. Another comrade had a barn in the neighborhood, so we slept there. At the time, many of our comrades were there in Kiustendil. A friend from Krichim, Stefan Manov, had also gone there after returning from Spain. On 9th September, together with some other comrades, he hoisted the black and red flag at the Krichim Train Station and at the canning factory. But the Bolsheviks would accept no other flag but their own.

After taking a bath in Kiustendil, we boarded a train. I was heading for Pernik, and Pencho to Kilifarevo. At the station in Zhabliano, some comrades saw us and more or less forcibly removed us from the train. They literally carried us into the village. It appeared they had been waiting for us. A feast had been set, but having been starved for so long, I had lost the habit of eating and could not take full advantage of the food offered. After a heartfelt parting from our comrades in Zhabliane, we left on the last train to Sofia. Night had descended when we reached Pernik. Pencho and I got off the train and headed to his grandfather Alexi's house, where my family had

taken refuge. My wife, however, had gone to my mother's in
Kosacha to prepare my memorial service! It was already 23rd
September, fourteen days since the coup, and they had given
up any hope for my safe return. When we were released, I had
asked one of the prison guards, a native of my home village,
to tell my mother that I was still alive and had joined the
Serbian partisans. However, he never passed the message on.

The next day I sent Pencho off to Kilifarevo while I headed
off to Kosacha by myself. I left the lice with Grandma Latina,
my wife's mother. Back home, it was a joyous welcome, with
hugs, kisses, and tears of joy. The memorial service was put
off for another time.

Back in Pernik, we initially moved in with my wife's parents. The house was very small so, not long after, we rented
a nearby room from 'Old' Doncho. He had built several small
cabins and supplemented his pension by renting these out.
The yard was overcrowded with young families but a small
room met our needs at the time. We used it as a bedroom,
a kitchen, and a guestroom. The problem was finding a job.
I was given a position at the Despatch Section at the mine,
where I was hired to work on the scales. But even before solving the problem of housing and work, I had got in touch with
comrades who had returned from the different fascist prisons
and camps. The events surrounding the coup had subsided.
The authority of the new power was being established. In
Pernik, we hurried to re-establish both the ideological and
the youth anarchist organizations. New comrades emerged,
as well as the older, more familiar ones. We founded a youth
organization and, at Maria Doganova's suggestion, named it
"Élisée Reclus". For the occasion, Maria wrote an excellent
article about the life and work of the great geographer. We
began campaigning to attract new members and supporters to
anarchism. This was easy at first. Some of the first members of
the youth organization were Anka Topalova, Emilia Lazarova,
Vera Sergieva, Maria Doganova, Elitsa Zaharinova, Kotse

Zaharinov, Alexander Nakov, Boyan Aleksov, Ivan Pavlov, Yordan (Dancho), Vasil and Boris Serginov, Getsa Serginova, Bozhichko Hristov and Yordan Georgiev. More young people joined later. The comrades in my native village had already managed to organize. We had no competition there and all the youth were with us. Milcho Slavov and Milcho Krumov were particularly active. Meetings were organized in order to properly explain anarchism.

At first, the Bolsheviks were not fully in control of the situation, so they tolerated us. We held regular meetings in rooms and apartments around Pernik. We did not yet need to hide from the authorities. But as early as the beginning of 1945, undercover police were already closely observing our activities. In order to undermine our influence, they first tried to pull some of the youth away from us with offers of work and education, and then with threats. Brutal action soon followed. The first victims were Dancho and Mariya. On their way from Kosacha to Pernik, they were stopped and severely beaten by a group of Bolsheviks. On 10ᵗʰ March 1945, ninety-two delegates were arrested at an anarchist conference being held in Kniazhevo. Our two representatives, Dimitur Vasilev and Yordan Georgiev, were among those arrested. After a two-week stay at a Home for the Blind, now converted into a prison, about half of those arrested were transferred to a concentration camp near Dupnitza. So, with us, the Bolsheviks began to apply forceful methods of "influence and persuasion" quite early on. Nevertheless, we had no intention of capitulating. We started holding our meetings outside the city and in remote locations near the Struma River or in the Golo Burdo area.

We established a support organization to aid our comrades in the camps, and to help their families with food, money and medicine. In the beginning, through connections among the guards, we could still get in touch with the anarchists in the camps. Incidentally, due to its proximity to the big camp at Kutzian, our organization in Pernik was assigned by the FACB* to establish and maintain relations with them. This task was not difficult for us. Some of our comrades worked in the same mine as the prisoners. Our most important liaison was the person known to the prisoners as 'Rope Boy'. This was Petur Neichev from Kosacha. He performed the tasks he had taken on with the greatest diligence.

Our organization assumed responsibility for distributing the Federation's organ, the newspaper, **Workers Thought**, as well as books and leaflets that FACB had managed to publish. **Workers Thought** quickly gained popularity and was distributed widely. But the new authorities did not like this in the least and they banned the paper. FACB was forced to publish its newsletter illegally.

In order to cut off anarchist ideas and influence, the Party mobilized its best agitators whom we called "anarcho-eaters". One of them, for example, was the notorious Ruben Levi, who traveled to cities and villages to refute the ideology of anarchism. To this end, he used obvious lies and slanders. But he met strong resistance of the kind that neither he, nor those who had assigned him this dirty job, had expected. Local anarchists, who asked him inconvenient questions, were well prepared and turned out to be more than a match for him. So, the effect was the opposite of what was intended and was positive for the anarchists. When the Bolsheviks realized they were losing the battle on the ideas front, they applied methods of force, including arrest and the concentration camp. Anarchists were among the first inhabitants in these establishments.

Meanwhile, in April, I got fired from my job for being "unreliable" and took a new job in the construction section of the mine. In the days that followed August 30 1945, it was a happier time for my family. We had a daughter who we named Yordanka, after her grandmother. Due to rationing,

---

* The Federation of Anarchist Communists in Bulgaria.

we experienced certain economic difficulties. We wasted time waiting in queues to obtain meager supplies. The black market existed but few were able to take advantage of this luxury. In 1945 the anarchist movement in our region had developed a truly mass character. In the towns of Radomir, Kiustendil, Dupnitsa, Blagoevgrad, and Sandanski, anarchists created their own organizations. I took every possible opportunity to visit these towns and most of the villages. Everywhere, the job of spreading anarchism, strengthening the organizations, and locating and disseminating the surviving literature, was in full swing. Because of the Bolshevik censorship, the Federation only managed to reissue Kropotkin's **The Conquest of Bread**. It also published several leaflets, among which I remember, **A History of May Day**.

In August 1945, we were able to restore the traditional anarchist youth fair in the Kitka area, which the fascists had banned in 1942. I want to give special attention to the history of this fair. In August 1933, a group of anarchists from the villages around Breznik (these included Laserman Asenov from Begunovtsi village and Atanas Tsenev, a teacher from Sadovik village) took a day-trip to the beautiful Kitka area near the monastery situated above Gigintsi village. With its wide green meadows and the dense shade of centuries-old oaks, it seemed an ideal place to gather together young people, organized anarchists, and sympathisers, in remembrance of the execution of Sacco and Vanzetti in the United States. After a grossly unfair trial, these two Italian anarchists had been sentenced to death and executed on 22nd August 1927, despite a wave of protests around the world. They were rehabilitated only posthumously, years later, and a film was made about them in Italy.

The idea was welcomed warmly and the commemoration grew into an annual progressive youth fair. Every year the number of participants increased. Thirty to forty people would come from some of the villages. Between eight hundred

and a thousand young people would gather at the fair! Not
all of them were anarchists, some were just sympathisers.
Some members of the Workers' Youth Union (RMS)* came
too, although they were not organized nor in large numbers.
Brief talks were presented and discussions were held on why
American "justice" had murdered two innocent workers.
There were recitals, singing, and music. Of course, there was
also the inevitable uniformed presence. The monarcho-fascist
authorities, concerned for the fair's orderly conduct, would
send a couple of police observers.

In 1936, I began to regularly attend the fair. I remember
one time, when I walked out onto the platform and recited
a poem by Heine†, *The Silesian Weavers*. It says, "A curse on
God!" and "A curse on the King!" When I finished, a police-
man who was standing nearby tried to arrest me. I slipped
into the crowd while the older comrades surrounded him to
explain to him who Heine was. The poor guy was so confused
he gave up any further attempt to catch me.

The fair was a convenient time to hold organizational
meetings and coordinating activities between the separate
organizations. It was easy for comrades to split off and hide
away from curious eyes. This continued until 1941. But some
newssheets spread by a small group of Bolsheviks gave the
authorities the long awaited excuse to ban the fair. We were
deprived of the opportunity to have a mass impact and work
legally among the youth from across this wide region.

In 1945, the year after the 9th September coup, the fair re-
sumed. Many young people gathered at Kitka on the arranged
day in August. Large groups came from Pernik, Radomir and
Breznik. We also invited the Workers' Youth Union members
from the region but only one group from Konska village came
to present a propaganda play for the upcoming elections.

And this is what happened the following year, 1946. Long

---

* A Communist Party youth organization.

† Heinrich Heine, 19th century German poet.

before the announced date, the Bolsheviks had tried to ruin the fair by leaning on some of our comrades with threats and blackmail. Their efforts were in vain as hundreds of young anarchists went to Kitka on the arranged date. A sizable group arrived from the youth organization in Sofia as well. This time there were no members of the Workers' Youth Union.

Our group from Pernik arrived near the monastery the night before. We set up camp under the big plum tree. At some point we saw a strange man approach. One of the comrades whispered to me that it was the District Constable of Radomir himself. I said that we should not let him know that we recognized him. The man asked us why we did not go inside the monastery. I replied that we traditionally spent the night under this tree. "Aren't you against traditions?" he argued. I disagreed, saying there were both good and bad traditions and we were only against the bad ones. This ambiguous dialogue did not last too long. It was late and some of the group complained that it was time for bed and the "conversation" could wait until the next day.

In the morning, groups started to arrive and the meadows around the monastery became thick with people. I remember the group from Begunovtsi village who numbered thirty-eight people led by a group of musicians. The youth from Kosacha arrived singing. Those who knew each other said their greetings, strangers were introduced, and before long, people were playing music and dancing. It was still early and young people were arriving individually. Along with Tzetza Germanova and one of our friends from Sofia, we decided that there was still time to go and get water from the monastery's fountain. There, sitting on benches in a fenced-off meadow, were about fifteen men, "hunters" with shotguns and all their hunting paraphernalia. I recognized two cops from Pernik among them, whose faces and names I remembered from my recent stay at the police station in Pernik. There was no doubt that the rest were their colleagues.

We returned to our comrades. We were just about to set the communal table when the "hunters" appeared. They looked at us closely, and then called up the three of us who had been at the water fountain. In the meantime, the boys were recognizing cops from Breznik, Radomir and other places. The Chief Constable of Radomir district introduced himself and said he was banning "the conference". He ordered everyone to return immediately to where they had come from. We tried to explain that there was no conference, and that this was a continuation of the same traditional fair that the fascist authorities and police had banned in 1942. We even invited him and his people to join us as we were just about to dine and have a good time. This was in vain. The cops and their superiors were adamant. Meanwhile, dozens of young people were gathering around us. One of them, Kircho, managed to whisper to me that there was a whole militia troop in the woods below the monastery, armed with sub-machine-guns and possibly awaiting a signal from the District Chief. The Radomir Chief Constable also quietly counselled with his people, then shouted that they were going to let us have our picnic. Voices of disagreement let him know that we rejected his "benevolence".

This, however, was our last gathering at our Kitka. For the anarchist movement, it was becoming increasingly difficult to conduct any legal activity.

Despite the obstacles the Bolsheviks put in our way, our work continued underground. In July 1946, our comrades in Radomir succeeded in calling a huge meeting for the 10th anniversary of the beginning of the revolution in Spain. The anarchists who spoke at this meeting were Petur Mihailov, a teacher, also a student Petur (whose last name I cannot remember), and the great orator, Manol Vasev, who the Bolsheviks poisoned in the Sliven prison. A Bolshevik and an Agrarian[*] also spoke at the meeting.

---

[*] From the Bulgarian Agrarian National Union (BANU).

After this meeting in Radomir, we tried to organize a similar event in Pernik, but the Bolsheviks did not allow us to do this, arguing that neither they nor we were to organize a meeting against Franco. But they were lying. Only a few days later they put up posters calling on the public to attend their meeting. After they had banned our speaker from participating in the event, we came up with a leafleting action. The leaflets, which we openly handed out and threw among the crowd, contained materials against Franco and his Falangists, but the Bolsheviks were offended that we had dared to participate without their permission. Maria Doganova was arrested the following day. A classmate of hers had seen her scattering leaflets and told her father, who had then gone to the militia*.

Next, after Maria, was Iliya Zdravkov, who denied his participation in the action and was beaten so severely that it took a long time for him to recover. The following day, Boyan Aleksov and I were arrested. We did not deny our participation but we were asked to say who in the organization was in contact with comrades in Dupnitsa, Kiustendil, Radomir, Breznik and Sofia. We refused to give any information whatsoever. For over 24 hours we were subjected to a severe beating. We were tortured with electric shocks. Whenever our legs got blue and swollen, they brought buckets of cold water and put our feet in them. More beatings followed. When they were finally convinced that they could not extract anything from us, we were released. From then on, I was called in frequently, with or without a reason.

The political situation in the country was deteriorating. The Bolsheviks were gradually beginning to get rid of their allies: Zvenarists†, Agrarians and social democrats. Of the Agrarians, they permitted only those who accepted their subordinate position of followers who were actually led by Communist infiltrators. Particularly, after the hanging of

---

* Under Bolshevism, the term 'militia' tended to replace the word 'police'.

† A right-wing military movement, see earlier note on Kimon Georgiev and Zveno (p. 4).

Nikola Petkov[*] in 1947, even the so-called "freedoms" were abolished and the prisons and concentration camps swelled and became overcrowded. The Kutzian concentration camp was transferred to a larger site at Bogdanov Dol. Continuing its activity at Kutzian, our organization again took on the task of establishing connections with comrades placed at Bogdanov Dol. This was not difficult for us because the prisoners worked at mines where our comrades were also employed. So the connection between Kutzian and Bogdanov Dol was strong. For the most part, we delivered letters and money between those in the camps and their families. Food was also brought in, but this could only be done in limited quantities. Instead, we gave food to the relatives of the detainees to take in to them at visiting times.

These were also the last years in Mikhail Gerdzikov's life[†]. Even though I knew a lot about this old revolutionary's history, I did not meet him until the winter of 1946-47. By then, he was confined to bed and under the care of his daughter, Magda. I visited him in their home. He was very pleased that young comrades were interested in him and his stories about the history of the movement. At a certain point, I noticed I was exhausting him with my questions. He gasped for breath, his pauses lasting increasingly longer. It was time to leave. As we parted, he gave me a pamphlet he had written years ago. The very title made a strong impression on me: **War or Revolution**.

In this pamphlet, he defends, from an anarchist viewpoint, the thesis that there is no just war and sees only the evil that wars bring to people. He argues that, at that time, "one of the most militarized countries is Bulgaria, a vast barracks, where only the voice of the Sergeant Major is heard" and that the working people have no external enemies but only internal ones, its masters who exploit it mercilessly. And if he had to go

---

[*] An Agrarian leader.

[†] A well-known Bulgarian anarchist.

to war, it is at them he would point his weapon. "Thus, against the army of violence there will rise the phalanxes of the discontented and the dispossessed, of the down-trodden, the robbed and the oppressed popular strata, and then the real war will begin, that which we desire and whose end will lead to the collapse of the current order. So, the people will answer the call for war with revolution, will put an end to this impossible situation and will launch a new era in which, freed from statism and clericalism, without god or master, the people will find complete happiness."

Alexander Nakov with his family: wife Kirilka Aleksova, holding son Marin, and Alexander Nakov is holding daughter Yordanka at 3 years. Radomir, 8 November, 1948.

Mikhail Gerdzhikov died on March 18 1947 at the age of 70. The Federation organized an impressive, well-attended funeral, with comrades attending from all corners of the country.

This funeral was the last public action of the Bulgarian anarchists. Soon after, the authorities began to fiercely persecute even the most insignificant activities of our comrades throughout the country. Terror and violence became the lasting characteristic of our society.

On March 6 1948 we had a son. It was a great joy. We named him Marin. Now, the family responsibilities became larger. Considering that only I was working, we were barely able to make ends meet.

Every day the Bolsheviks' brutality towards people with different ideas increased. In order to be among other people and to exert influence in some way, we joined the existing Temperance and Esperanto societies, in which anarchists and anarchist sympathisers had previously been a majority. During very heavy rain in June 1948, the River Struma broke its banks and flooded much of the neighborhood to the east of Pernik's thermal power plant. Our home was also flooded, with the water reaching the height of the windows. At the time, I had gone to the village while my wife had stayed alone with the children. With the help of our neighbors everybody managed to get out and find shelter with one of my wife's cousins. The property, however, was now completely uninhabitable. About sixty families whose homes had suffered flood damage were allowed to settle in the school in the Tvurdi Livadi neighborhood. I do not know if anyone can imagine how one can "settle" with small children and no furniture, directly on the bare wooden floor of a school. There was no hot water, nor any facilities at all.

I was working at the construction department at the time, in the stores. Everyone knew about my accommodation problems. One of the masons told me that a block of about thirty flats, belonging to the mine, had recently been completed in the Tvurdi Livadi district. Management was supposed to give them to the needy. When I found out that we, who had suffered flood damage, were not considered "needy", I took a bunch of keys, went to the block and unlocked all the apartments. I made some calculations and realized that we could not have a separate apartment for each family. Each apartment had two rooms and a kitchen with a brick stove. The solution was to settle two families into each apartment.

I went back to the school, gathered the men, the heads of families, in a room and told them about the block of flats and how we were going to settle there. My suggestion was accepted unanimously. We made arrangements that the families could pick who to share an apartment with. We even tossed coins to decide who would occupy which apartment number. So early one morning, the illegal settlement began.

The next day I was called to the head office at the mine to explain who had given me permission to allocate the apartments. They were designated for employees who had long been waiting for company housing. We had a huge row. Finally, I said to them, "Throw us out if your conscience will let you." They did not evict us but they complained about me to the militia. This time, however, after I had explained the circumstances, the militia let me go. I never did find out which of the families I had arranged housing for had grassed me up in gratitude for having a room for his family.

Hard times followed for our movement. We continuously received news of arrests, searches, beatings, and other tortures. Some of our more active comrades, among them those with international renown and connections, managed to flee the country. One of these was Georgi Hadzhiev. Ivan Rachev, who had the courage to write the book **Ten Months' Persecution of Anarchists,** was also able to flee. An overall estimate of those who saved themselves by fleeing abroad comes to about 100.

At home, the Fifth Congress of the Party was approaching. The Bolsheviks were storming ahead.

CHAPTER 7: 16ᵗʰ DECEMBER

On December 16 1948, early in the morning at around five o'clock, I heard a loud knock on the door. "Open up! Militia!" When I opened the door, I saw a plain-clothes and two uniformed militia men with rifles and knives standing at the door. "You are under arrest!" said the plain-clothes cop. I barely had the time to get dressed. The cop hurried me so I did not get the chance to say goodbye to my wife and children, who had woken up and were standing there, petrified by the scene. I was not allowed to take anything with me. They took me into detention at the State Security in Pernik. They had already picked up virtually all of the anarchists from Pernik who were on their lists, including the women. The newly-wed Tsvetana Draganova was there, as well as Maria Doganova, who had also just got married. They both ended up spending their honeymoons in jail. A few days later, Maria Vasileva was also brought in, arrested because the cops had been unable to find her husband.

We learned later that on the same day, 16ᵗʰ December 1948, anarchists from all over the country had been arrested. The "power of the people" had started its retribution on the anarchist sons of the people.

We were in custody, waiting day after day with no news, no visits and no charges against us, except for the fact that we belonged to one movement and believed in one idea. From time to time, someone would be called for interrogation. They kept most of us in one room. Unfortunately, it was a severe winter, which made our situation even more difficult. The taps were frozen and there was no water for drinking or washing. Food was brought from outside by our parents and relatives, but the food remained uneaten. Water was a much greater necessity but we had no means of communicating with our relatives and they could not have imagined we would be left without water! This went on for 31 days. Over time, comrades from all over the country passed through the temporary detention centre in Pernik, on their way to the concentration camps at Kutsian and Bogdanov Dol. Maria kept asking the new arrivals if they had any news of her husband, Jack. One morning, thirty-one days later, we were driven to the Bogdanov Dol camp while the women were sent off to the Dobrudzha region.

At the camp we were greeted by the notorious blood-sucking Gershanov. His first word when addressing us was "Vermin!"

The rooms were furnished with two-tier bunk-beds. During our stay at the State Security prison, we had been attacked by swarms of lice. Here though, we had something good. There was a caldron in which we placed our clothes for delousing.

At the camp we all became miners. I was assigned by Gershanov to work at the pit as a coal digger. Later I got to do all the specialized mining jobs.

Prior to our arrival, at the mine and also at the camp, many of our anarchist acquaintances had already been brought in from around the country. As older inmates, they immediately sought to make contact with the newcomers in order to offer help. We worked in three shifts. The mine was located a kilometre from the camp. I was attached as assistant to a more experienced digger. Many of the detainees had never seen a mine before and I found their fear of their first entry into the pit odd. I had an agronomist friend who got so scared that he started screaming, "There's no way out of here!" It was scary indeed. The coal faces were deep and narrow, it was dark and there was not enough air. There were army officers among us who had been fearless in the front line of the Tsar's army, but they were quite overwhelmed here.

Anyone who failed to meet their quota, which was the amount an experienced miner could be expected to produce, was made to spend the night standing under the lamp post in the yard. That was only one of the punishments. Others were determined by the personal inclinations and imagination of the management. Three of the managers stood out as particularly cruel bullies. These were Handzhiev (the civilian Chief of Camp), Captain Gershanov, and Petur Gogov. Those three would beat us with or without a reason. Handzhiev was the cruelest. Once he jumped on someone and would not stop. There was also one so-called "supervisor" called Poshtadzhiev*. His job was to recruit spies from among the frightened detainees, who would then grass up their mates. He promised the informers early release, which, by the way, never happened.

Upon our arrival at the camp, we were given old discarded police and military uniforms and rubber sandals. Dressed in this way, we looked like scare-crows. The food usually consisted of cabbage, leeks, and potatoes. We very rarely had meat. At least we were given "miners' bread"†, which was satisfying to an extent. Visits were allowed only on 1st May and 9th September‡. During my whole stay at Bogdanov Dol, I had only one visit from my wife and two children. My son, Marin, had turned one year old and was trying to walk, and my daughter, Yordanka, had turned three. The visit lasted only ten minutes. I next saw my wife and children four years later when I returned from Belene concentration camp.

I had acquaintances from the villages around Pernik working at the pit and they agreed that I could send and receive letters through them to and from my family. Zdravko (I don't remember his last name) and Boris Bogdanov, a mining technician from the Leskovets village, were always ready to do all kinds of favours.

Everything attested to the "culture" of Gershanov the Bloodsucker but particularly absurd were his "speeches"

---

* The name means "Mr Postal".
† This is a large, dark loaf.
‡ May Day and the day of the Bolshevik coup.

to the "flock". For example, on May 24 1949, he opened his
speech like this, "Today, all over all globe and here in Bulgaria, people are celebrating the day of the brothers Cyril
and Methodius."*

What bothered me most in the mine was all the dust
smoke that formed after the detonation of explosives in
the coal seams. To this day, I feel disgust in the company of
smokers. Because of our intolerance to smoke, several other
comrades and I were eventually moved to another pit where
no explosions were being carried out at the time. I worked
the lift there. There were four of us on the lift: me, Dimitur
Iv. Stoev, Milan Drenchev, and one whose name I do not
remember, plus a militia guard.

One night, when we were working the third shift, we were
getting ready for our break around midnight. There were four
of us in the shed where the lift was located. Milan Drenchev
said he was going to the water pump near the pit entrance to
wash his hands. I also went out after Milan and saw him take
off his greatcoat, but instead of going to the pump, he went
towards the road. The militia guard was dozing behind the
shed. I went back in. After some time had passed, Dimitur
Stoev became concerned. He sent me to the water pump to see
why Drenchev was taking so long. When I came back, I told
him that there was no sign of Drenchev. He got really worried
and wanted to tell the guard straight away that Drenchev had
disappeared. I persuaded him to wait in case Drenchev had
run away, and this would give him time to get further away.
Stoev agreed with me and went to the militia guard about
two hours later and said, "Milan is running away. Look, he's
over there behind the willows. Fire a shot. Raise the alarm."
The guard, a young boy, did not have the courage to shoot.
He announced the escape only in the morning, after we had
got back to the camp.

* Saints Cyril and Methodius were two Byzantine diplomats, Christian
missionaries, and creators of the Cyrillic alphabet.

They first called Dimitur Stoev, then me. When I entered Gershanov's office (aka the thrashing room), he hit the table with his fist so hard that the ink-pot flew across the room all the way to the door. "Vermin, vermin, vermin! Tell me why you let him escape?" He was ready to jump on me like a wild animal. I replied, "The militiaman did not dare shoot at him, so who am I to stop him?" Then again, "Vermin, vermin, vermin! Get out!"

I found out later that the militia guard was fired because of this incident, but this was six months later, when I was already at Belene and had bumped into Milan Drenchev himself. I asked him why he was there. He said that he had been caught hiding in a cornfield while trying to cross the border.

Towards the end of 1949, when the camp had become swollen with people, some of the old inmates from this camp were sent to others throughout the Bulgarian Gulag. More and more new inmates were being delivered every day. After the death of the mass murderer Georgi Dimitrov* many people were brought in because they had not been crying! Others were brought in because they had laughed, and others still because they would not say who had laughed and who did not cry. We called these people "gravediggers".

Towards the end of March 1950, after a fourteen month stay at Bogdanov Dol, about 300 of us were loaded onto horse wagons and taken to the Belene-Nikopol irrigation system. Once there, we were given shovels, picks, wooden handcarts and wheel-barrows. We were told that there was an urgent need for drainage and irrigation canals, so we were assigned to a labour unit. An overseer, who was always drunk, determined our daily quotas each morning. Gradually, the quotas grew so big that it was not possible to fulfill them. We worked from sunrise to sunset, guarded by militia from Vratsa. We lived in an enormous tent, something like a circus big-top. At night, a wheel-barrow was placed in front of the tent to

* The first Bolshevik leader of Bulgaria.

serve as the toilet. If someone wanted to use the toilet, he had to shout in loud voice, "Mr. Militiaman, I'm going for a number one" (or for a number two, respectively). But this loud shouting would wake up those sleeping. In the end, it was nearly impossible to get enough sleep. There were also some comical situations. There was a German among us. Once when he shouted, the militiaman did not like his accent, so he asked him, "What's your name?" and our guy replied, "Walter Arthur Kleinemann." "Say your name in Bulgarian!" The German repeated his name. "In Bulgarian, you mother!" Since Walter could not come up with a Bulgarian name for himself, he was not allowed to use the wheel-barrow, so he wet his pants.

There was also one man with cancer who screamed so loudly with pain that everyone was kept awake. Management did not give one single pill for pain relief to this man.

CHAPTER 8: THE BELENE CONCENTRATION CAMP

When we finished the work, we were lined up into rows and a section of the Vratsa militia drove us to Persin Island, already infamous among us. After a three hour journey, we found ourselves on the banks of the peaceful Danube. We got into several large boats, each with two oarsmen who rowed us to the bank opposite Persin. After a short journey, we arrived at the so-called 1st Work Site. We were shoved into shacks made of whatever materials were to hand. The walls were constructed from stakes and woven willow poles. The roofs were grass-covered, while small openings in the walls served as windows. When it rained, the inside would initially remain dry, but before long, the water would begin to drip through the roof, and long after the rain had stopped outside, the inside would still be flooded.

They split us up into work-brigades, gave us tools and took us to uproot willow trees. They had prepared work quotas, i.e. a certain number of people were assigned per tree depending on the diameter of its trunk. The people who had been brought here before us had already rooted out large areas which were immediately levelled and put to use as crop planting areas. Rapeseed, sunflower, corn, hemp, and all varieties of wheat were being sown. After almost a month, they moved me to the 2nd Work Site. The shacks there were much the same, only made more skillfully, and what is most important, the roofs were tiled. At first, we uprooted willows there again. Then we were moved to the farm.

There were people doing everything there. We did the hoeing to plant sunflowers, corn, potatoes, pumpkins, and melons. The soil was alluvial and needed no fertilization. Production was substantial. From a hectare of tomato plants they harvested 18 tons of produce. The hemp plants were so tall that when the militiamen rode through them on horseback, neither the horse nor the rider could be seen. Everything grew in abundance.

Despite this abundance, we were constantly being tortured with indescribable hunger. The bread rations were 420g when we worked and 360g when we did not work. There was nothing there we did not eat. At first we caught the turtles, then the frogs and the snakes, and, of course, this was only when someone was lucky enough to run into one of these reptiles. We did not overlook the cats and dogs that had the misfortune to come here.

According to camp regulations, everyone was entitled to receive a food package of up to 10kg once in three months; and also once in three months, to write one letter of up to seven lines and to receive one letter. On 1st May and 9th September, visits were allowed. During the four years I spent at Belene, I had one visit from my mother. All the letters I wrote saying that I was allowed to have visits were collected in the post by the Pernik cops and never reached my family. Whenever I asked camp management why no one came to visit me, I was told that my relatives did not want to come and see me. And when my wife asked about visiting me, she was told I did not want to invite her.

As for the packages, camp management almost always found excuses to deprive me of them. Such a punishment for some inmates was almost the equivalent of a death sentence. But among the anarchists, the food packages were split between everyone, giving priority to the sick and the weak, those recently punished and those who were lucky enough to survive solitary confinement. In 1951, the majority of deaths were due to starvation, far more than deaths due to shootings or beatings with clubs, which provoke such authentic horror for innocent contemporary readers of memoir prose.

When the guards wanted to destroy someone, there were less bloody ways to do this. They would send the person to "Tel Aviv" – this was the name we had given the lock-up because it was tightly surrounded by barbed wire. I also had the "pleasure" of visiting this godly establishment. Inside, there was a single plank by the wall for sitting on and lying down. The floor was soaked with water and mud. The food was 360g of bread and a ladle of hot water per day. After fifteen days, having barely survived this hell, you would be sent straight back to work. And pity the ones who were unable to fulfill their work quotas. They would be immediately returned to Tel Aviv, and they would never leave it until they were carried out feet first.

When I got out of Tel Aviv, the comrades greeted me with food, but when we went to hoe the sunflowers, I was unable to keep hold of the hoe. I survived thanks solely to the mutual aid among us anarchists, which has always been not only a simple human principle but a well-organized practice. One comrade stood on my right side, another stood on my left, and as they hoed their lines, they hoed mine too. I pretended to work. Within several days, I was back on track with the work norm.

At one point the island got quite overcrowded. There were about 4,000 people spread across the different sites. The political composition of the inmates was approximately the following: about 1,500 Agrarians, 600 anarchists, a few social democrats, Ratniks, Branniks and Legionnaires*, a few former officers, former policemen, a handful of priests, several former ministers, a group of Greeks who had refused to fight for the Bolsheviks, and even a few Bolsheviks who had made errors with "the Party and the people". Yet all of these diverse groups were there because of principles or ideas. So, for me, the saddest group was also the largest, the simple discontented peasants who had dared to ask why they had been deprived of their ox, horse or donkey.

We worked hard at the sites and the administration worked no less hard than us. Every night they would call a few of the

---

* Ratniks were Bulgarian orthodox, Branniks were monarchists and Legionnaires were national socialists.

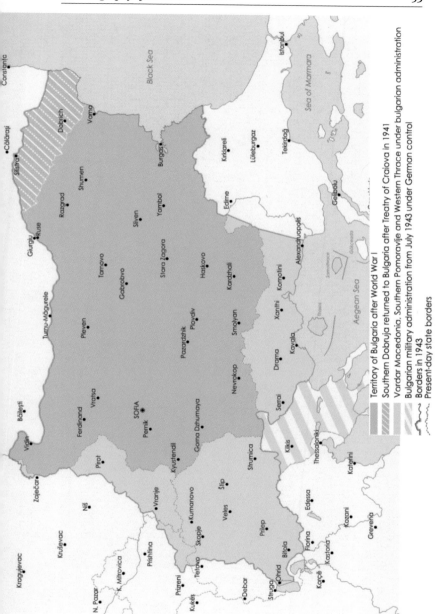

Territory of Bulgaria after World War I

Southern Dobruja returned to Bulgaria after Treaty of Craiova in 1941

Vardar Macedonia, Southern Pomoravlje and Western Thrace under bulgarian administration

Bulgarian military administration from July 1943 under German control

Borders in 1943

Present-day state borders

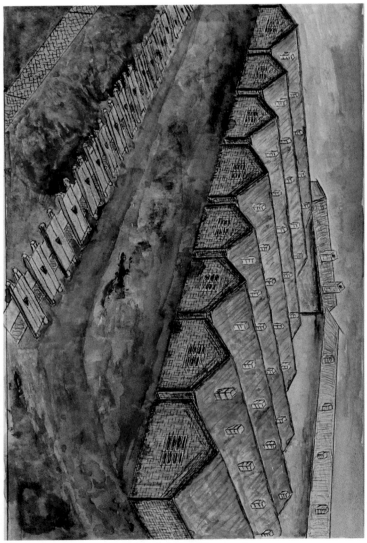

Latrine for 5,000 people.

The dike at Worksite #2.

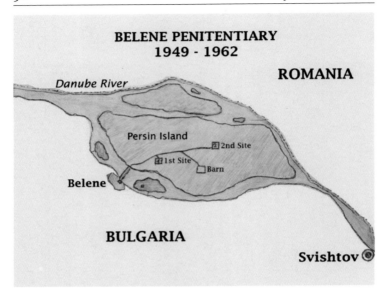

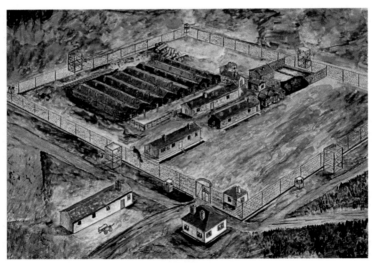

Worksite #2 (1950–1960)

inmates, specially selected, and would condition them night after night to become informers, with the sweet promise that they would be released at the earliest opportunity. But first, they had to prove they deserved the trust of the Party by informing on their comrades, on whose backs they would earn their release. The administration used all means to demoralize us, and spread fear and insecurity. So, in addition to the hard labour, starvation and bullying, they also tried to influence us psychologically. To this end, of course, as with the previous camp, there was a full-time "supervisor" whose task it was to do just that, to condition and provide informers.

The eating area was located outside in the yard. The wicker tables were made from woven willow branches. We ate there in the cold, rain, snow and storms. Occasionally, sweets or waffles were delivered to the canteen. So, to buy one lev's worth of sweets, you had to stand in line for hours. The smokers were the only ones who could not complain about a poor supply. If someone working in the garden or melon field tried to taste what he produced, God help him! The lock-up, Tel Aviv, awaited him. At first, we drank water straight from the Danube, but later, we began digging wells.

The spring floods were the hardest to survive through. The entire island became flooded except for the place where the 2nd Work Site was situated. It was as if nature had purposefully built a slope where the huts, oven and kitchen were situated.

Once we had cleared nearly all the willows, management took care that we should not remain idle, and ordered us to build a dike around the entire island to protect it from floods. With the primitive technology, wooden handcarts, shovels, picks, and even without any wheel-barrows, we started to build large embankments. The quotas were impossible, the hunger was unbearable. This was how yet another Bolshevik site was to be completed. I do not believe the Egyptians endured such hunger and misery while digging the Suez Canal. Many people had given up all hope that this hell would ever be over. Bearing in mind what I already knew about Siberian camps, I started thinking about the fascist gas chambers, where people were killed in seconds. No, the Bolsheviks were definitely more merciful. They sent people to have their physical and moral strength drained at the Gulag sites. The slaughter was done in a more civilized manner.

After all the camps were concentrated into one, on Belene Island, it was time to "hide" the women from all around, too. They were moved from the concentration camps at Nozharevo and Bosna to the tiny island of Shturcheto*. Most were taken there because of their political views: Agrarians, anarchists, Trotskyists. There were actresses and intellectuals among them. These women lived in the most miserable conditions. They worked breeding pigs.

About some of our comrades who were in prison, one could (and must!) write, not only short memoirs but whole novels. For me, these comrades are Vasil 'The People' Todorov and Hristo Kolev Yordanov.

When Vasil Todorov received his diploma after graduating from school, he destroyed it before reaching home. It would have helped to get him a civil service job, i.e. to serve the very institution he intended to fight against. He preferred to be a worker, and became a printer. He learned the trade, worked and read widely. Then began the ordeal of moving from prison to prison, first during the fascist regime and immediately after, the Bolshevik one. While we were at Skopje prison, he argued endlessly with the Bolsheviks. There were always topics for debate, such as the Paris Commune, Makhno, Kronstadt, the Spanish Revolution, and Botev[†]. He used to warn our comrades, that if the Bolsheviks take power in our country after this war, there would be dark days ahead. He was right. We were all thrown into the camps and prisons. Vasil was picked up in the very first months and became one

---

* Shturcheto translates as 'the Cricket'.

† Hristo Botev, revolutionary and poet.

of the first inhabitants of the concentration camps. He did not get involved with starting a family but devoted his entire life to the struggle for the ideals of justice and freedom. He remained a fighter to his very last breath.

We called Hristo Kolev 'The Great' but not because of any association with or adherence to Levski[*] or because of his physical and intellectual qualities, but simply because there was another comrade with the exact same name, Hristo Kolev 'The Small'. The Great was a student of Vasil Todorov's and was one of his best followers, in every respect. His early years were a time of struggle and risks. He was expelled from university twice and did not complete his higher education. Three times he was engaged as editor of the newspaper, **Workers' Thought**. Three times he was tried and convicted under the State Defence Act. All this, of course, took place before 9th September 1944. After that date, he spent over 10 years in different prisons and camps in the Bolshevik Gulag. He was interned in Balvan, Pet Mogili and Polski Trumbesh. Only in 1984 was he finally freed from this idyllic exile.

In the fascist prisons and the Bolshevik prisons and camps, The Great was just like Vasil Todorov, indomitable and relentless in arguments with his ideological opponents. No one dared enter into a serious argument with him. However, he was also the person to receive the cruelest treatment: severe beatings, solitary confinement and deprivation of food and visitors. His unbreakable spirit overcame all of this. The Agrarian poet, Yosif Petrov, dedicated the following poem, **The Stoic**, to him:

The Stoic

To Hristo Kolev

**When dark fate gathered us together
in the concentration camp by the white Danube,**

---

[*] The historic Bulgarian revolutionary, Vasil Levski, known as "the apostle of freedom".

in cells and dungeons
you spent years locked up.
Yet you were young with cheerful eyes,
handsome and well-built,
generous in courage and heroism
but sparing of words.
Our labour camp was reliant
on your strength and morality;
without these it would have been terrible,
with so much man-made mud!
You burned the mud-slingers
with your red-hot speech,
and for informers you were
death itself – with scythe and sword.
Many a scoundrel did you scorch,
and defeated, they kept their silence.
Even among the evil guards
you instilled respect and fear!
With the oppressed you were kind and warm,
with the oppressor, cold as ice!
I never heard you wail or moan,
even while you were mercilessly oppressed.
To you fate was cruel
and heavy was your earthly burden,
but a lofty ideal
kept you warm in the struggle.
Physically strong. Sharp-witted.
Insanely brave. Pure in heart.
A final touch to a wonderful portrait –
a titan of the struggle. An anarchist.

This is how I remember you,
this is how you are still today: a stoic,
seasoned and hard as steel,
with a sharp tongue and strong in spirit.
Manly, clear-eyed, calm,

as if staring at another world;
as a shining example you deserve
to be cast whole in bronze.
A man exiled, sent
by a spiteful ruler, vicious and savage;
you, our hero hundredfold,
wither away like a living ember.
I am glad that in that hard labour camp
I was alongside you,
and you and I, in that human suffering,
shared food together.
And looking back at your path
I stand before you, in honour
I lower my brow
before your great deeds.

— *Yosif Petrov, 1980*[*]

After November 1989, Hristo Kolev actively participated in the restoration of the Federation of Anarchists in Bulgaria (FAB). He sold his apartment in Polski Trumbesh and donated the total amount received towards the purchase of a home for the FAB in Sofia. This action surprised no one. It was a natural thing to do for the man who had devoted his whole life in the service of a great ideal. Today, this new home continues to shelter the organization's active centre.

After the death of the mass murderer ("the Father of the People"), the camp regime softened. They started releasing prisoners, at first selectively, then later en masse, with a group being released almost daily. I was released on 10th August 1953. I had spent almost one Bolshevik "Five-Year Plan" in hell.

---

[*] Translator's note. Divided into two sections, *The Stoic* consists of thirteen quatrains with a rhyming scheme of ABAB in the Bulgarian original. The stresses are varied and the poem makes frequent use of syntactical inversions which contribute to the rhythm. However, such poetic devices fall outside the scope of this book and the above is only a rough translation, intended to give the reader the general flavour of the poem.

A comrade from the Dupnitsa area, Ivan Karaliiski, was released with me, as well as an ex-cop, whose name was Vasil. We were handed packages containing our civilian clothes. But as we got dressed, we discovered that, after five years in these packages, our clothes were now all moth-eaten and completely unwearable. There were no other clothes. However, I got dressed, safe in the knowledge that I looked even worse than my grandma's old scarecrow. When we got to the train station in Belene,

My sister, Vetka.

Karaliiski and I realized we had no money for the ticket. We had to ask to borrow the fare from the cop. Because we had all been released together, he gave us 50 lev apiece. As soon as we got home, we hurried to send the money back to him by postal order.

Upon arriving in Sofia, we went to the barber's shop across the street from the station. The people there stared at us as if we were aliens from an unknown but certainly uncivilized planet. When it was my turn to sit in the chair, the barber asked in a whisper where we had come from. I, however, responded loud enough for everyone in the shop to hear it, "From Belene." After she had cut my hair and given me a shave, I asked how much I owed her. She quietly replied, "Nothing."

When the train reached Razpredelenie station in Pernik, I got off while Ivan Karaliiski continued on to his village, Slatino near Dupnitsa. I did not get off at Pernik's central station because I did not want to pass through the town centre looking the way I did. I took roads where I would meet fewer people. Eventually, I ended up in my wife's grandfather's and my father-in-law's yard, where I saw three boys playing. I tried to recognize which one was my son. One of them seemed a bit too tall, the other one too short, so I guessed that the one in the middle could be my Marin. When I approached the kids, as soon as they saw me they ran away, disappearing into the neighborhood. For more than two weeks, my son was not able to accept me. The other two boys were the sons of my brother-in-law, Boyan Aleksov, who had got out of the camp before me.

Grandma Latinka greeted me. My daughter had gone to Kosacha to stay with my mother, and my wife was at work. First off, Grandma Latinka gave me a change of clothes so as not to scare the children.

Two days later, I went to Kosacha village to see my daughter, Yordanka. At first, when she looked at me, she was also a little bit frightened, but she quickly came to accept me.

CHAPTER 9: AFTER THE CONCENTRATION CAMPS

O nce I had seen my family, I started looking for work. However, wherever I went, I was rejected once they had seen my record. One day, I went to the hiring officer, Milen Dimov, at the Minstroy Works, who I had known from before 9th September. When I told him I had returned from the camps but could not find work, he said there was an opening at their firm. I wrote a covering letter and curriculum vitae and went to the Teva mine, where the railway maintenance facility was. I was hired in a crew consisting entirely of unreliable people like me. The foreman was Raicho Yordanov from Rezhantsi village, who had returned from Belene before me. I worked there for one year but the work was too hard for my post-camp physique and it was also poorly paid.

I sought a position at a more lucrative transport enterprise. The head there was my sister Vetka's husband, Vasil Duparanov. He was a cobbler by trade, having only finished the fourth grade at school. When I asked him if, as a poorly educated person, he did not fear being harmed by a report or a plan, he smiled and told me that every document he signed was signed by at least three others before him, so he would be the last person to be harmed.

I worked at this enterprise for a year and a day. I did not leave of my own will. Two days earlier, I had been sent to unload wagons of charcoal at the Pernik thermal power plant. On the third day, I was stopped at the gate. I was told that the Ministry of the Interior had ordered them to turn me away. I left the site and complained to my brother-in-law (the manager) that I was not allowed to go to work. He shrugged his shoulders and told me that he was unable to help. I was forced to return to rail maintenance, but this time at the Republic metal mine.

Before taking this job, I tried to get hired at the machine-building plant. A hiring officer even gave me a note saying he would take me on in a few days. In the meantime, a Bolshevik who was familiar with my attitude to their principles had seen me looking for work at the plant. When I went back to see the hiring officer who had personally promised to take me on, he told me that there was no work for me at the plant. I reached inside the inside pocket of my jacket to show him the note he had given me. He panicked, picked up the phone, and frantically screamed, "Militia!" He probably thought I was reaching for a weapon. Meanwhile, a long queue of job applicants had formed at his door. Upon hearing the officer's scream, they stormed into the office to save him. This happened exactly in the days when Hungarian workers and citizens had risen against their "beloved Party". I went to the plant manager to protest against the discrimination against me. However, he had been informed of my identity in advance and told me that "one rotten apple spoils the barrel"*. It was obvious that the events in Hungary had caused widespread panic, and fear and spite had also overtaken our managers. After this happened, I gave up trying to find a job in town. I was forced to seek work in the outskirts only, so the old acquaintances would not notice me.

My life was gradually returning to normal after I began working at the railway maintenance unit at the Republic mine. I was a diligent worker; I never received any negative comments about my performance. After a year in rail maintenance, I enrolled on a course in train mechanics. I passed the exam with distinction. Initially, I worked as a train mechanic, then later I became a wagon inspector. As a railway worker, I was already entitled to free train tickets for all of the train lines. So I made good use of them.

I had already been in touch with all the anarchist comrades

---

* In the original, the phrase used is "a sour pot needs little to make it ferment".

in Pernik who had returned from the concentration camps and prisons. I want to mention the names of some of them who deserve to be remembered: Dimitur Vasilev, who did time in many a fascist prison and Bolshevik camp and who became ill with leukemia; Neno A. Katsarski, firm, incorruptible and very active in spreading anarchist ideas; Laserman Asenov Minev, ideologically well-versed; Atanas Iliev Kisyov from Kalimantsi village, who returned after finishing his sentence; his brother-in-law Ivan Baltov, who also returned from prison; Boyan Aleksov Stefanov, who lay in prison before 9th September, and then later in the Bolshevik camps, where he became ill and was released due to sickness; and Boyan 'The Granny' Ivanov, an older, mellow comrade. Unfortunately, there were also people such as Boris Serginov and his wife Getsa, who renounced their beliefs. These, however, were few.

Some comrades were in a state of extreme distress. Some were ill, having lost their health in the Bolshevik camps. These people needed financial and moral support. We began collections in order to assist those in need. Understandably, such activity was a thorn in the side of the "People's State". Its "People's Militia" did not rest as long as it had a job to do. No matter how cautious and careful I was, I had the constant feeling (which later on turned out to be quite justified) that there was always someone behind me with "clean hands and a cool head"*. In those days, whoever I saw or spoke to would be summoned to the "comrades" at the militia station and forced to give a written explanation of what we had discussed. He would then be forced to sign an additional declaration saying that he would tell me nothing of what had happened. The militia never contacted me personally. Luckily for me, some of those called in by the militia were honest and conscientious people. Three of them told me all about the interrogations. These were Mihail Pchelinski, an engine driver; Metodi Mlad-

---

* Here, the author seems to echo the old Cheka/KGB motto, which says, "the Chekist is a man with a warm heart, a cool head and clean hands".

enov, a dental technician; and Petur from Kakas village, an assistant engine driver. A neighbour regularly informed me when cops had been to interrogate her husband and what they had asked about me.

Traveling at weekends with my free train tickets, I was able to get in touch with comrades from almost every part of the country. Of course, and I learned this only after I had finally seen an extract from my dossier, this activity was also noted by the cops.

I will tell you a bit about my work at the Republic mine. The plans and quotas there were somewhat ambitious. So, with this in mind, the engineers, technicians, hiring personnel and the various types of overseer were never satisfied with the results and always wanted more and more. Industrial accidents occurred constantly, with a substantial number of victims. There were these antiquated Soviet wagons, known as "ladybugs", which were real killers of railway workers. The track was repaired with whatever materials were at hand. So, the wagons were unstable and became derailed regularly. I enjoyed a degree of respect from my colleagues and other workers at the mine. One colleague there, Sasho from Lev-ski*, monitored me closely. There was also an official State Security representative appointed at the mine, I think his name was Velinov, who carefully watched my every move and every communication with the other workers.

In early October 1971, a great comrade, Dimitur Vasilev, passed away. We organized an impressive funeral for him. Comrades from Sofia, Pernik, Radomir, Dupnitsa, Samokov, Kiustendil and the nearby villages were invited; and they came. After describing his life, I mentioned that, as an an-archist, he had been through fascist prisons and Bolshevik camps. This speech of mine was reported word for word to State Security by someone I trusted. Because of this funeral, several comrades and I were later arrested. I spent 31 days

* The football club.

at Razvigor Street* in Sofia under continuous interrogation. They had become more "civilized" and didn't beat me but, unaccountably, I never spent two nights in the same cell. They wanted me to tell them who I had invited to the funeral and who had attended, as if they had not counted them already. They had evidence that I had been distributing books and brochures with anarchist content. I denied everything but I had to pay for saying at the funeral that Vasilev was an anarchist and that this was courageous. And paid I did.

---

* The location of the Central State Security Bureau.

CHAPTER 10: EXILED

I was exiled from Pernik to a village near Razgrad, Topchii, for a period of five years. Two other comrades were exiled with me, Atanas Kisyov and Liuben Dzhermanov, because they had also said that Vasilev was an anarchist. Until I could find a room to rent in Topchii, I slept in a basement at the Town Hall that had been designated for prisoners. I found lodgings with a good family. My landlords were 'Old' Hristo and 'Mother' Rada. At the time, tomatoes, peppers and other garden vegetables were in season. But one day, after I had bought some vegetables from the village greengrocer's, Mother Rada scolded me for not picking vegetables from her abundant garden but buying from the store, and thus embarrassing her as a host.

My wife and children came to visit me three times while I lived in Topchii. Each time they visited, Mother Rada would kill a turkey to cook. The 15 lev rent I was paying could not have been enough to pay for one of these turkeys, if I were to buy one.

I was fairly content with my lodgings but there was nowhere for me to work. The village Mayor and the neighborhood militiaman frequently reminded me that I should have been working. The only work one could get in the village was at a quarry and at the village farm. I refused categorically to work at either of these places.

One day I was called to the State Security offices in Razgrad. The Major, head of State Security, asked me why I did not want to work in the village. I replied that I had worked all my life and I would still work but I was hoping to be offered a suitable job. I told him that I was a technician. He turned out to be much more agreeable than the cops in Pernik, since he promised to check for suitable work and let me go. Just three days later, he ordered the local militiaman to have me collect my belongings and go on to him. It was a Monday in July, 1974.

I left for Razgrad, having parted with my good landlords. The head of State Security and one of his subordinates, Georgiev, put me in a jeep and drove me to Samuil train station. From there, we went to a wagon-building plant which was still under construction on one side. On the other side, there were workshops ready for repairing four-axle wagons. They introduced me to the manager, a young man, intelligent and very polite. He just asked me a few questions then told me to submit a job application the following day, dated from today, and my curriculum vitae. Then the cops and I got back in the jeep and they drove off along a steep road covered with pot-holes and rocks.

An hour later, we reached the village of Huma. The cops stopped by the village pub and asked the pub landlord to bring a bag of ammonium nitrate from the collective farm. The bag was delivered and its contents poured into a large tub, which was then filled with water, and finally, a case of beer was placed in it to cool. It was a little after noon. As we sat there, the big names from the whole village came to greet us: the Mayor, the school principal, the post office chief, the village doctor, a teacher and two others. There were ten of us at the table. By the evening, we had eaten everything there was to be found on the pub shelves. We drank several cases of beer. I, who at weddings would just have one beer in company, now drank three bottles. Once the cops were plastered, they ordered the Mayor to find a room for me, before staggering their way into the jeep. The pub bill was paid by the village dignitaries. The cops and I were treated as guests, in other words, we did not pay.

In the evening, the doctor accompanied me to the surgery and accommodated me in a small room used for the sterilization of needles and other such processes. There was a bed, a table and a chair. Everyone in the pub spoke excellent Bulgarian so I had not realized that there was not a single Bulgarian in the village. The doctor told me that the women there wore a kind of loose pantaloons, known as shalvar*. Initially, I was worried about the language barrier but this feeling did not last long. Only the smaller children, the elderly and those who had not been to school did not know Bulgarian. Everyone was friendly and treated me kindly. They were very sociable. On their way back from the melon patch or the allotment, the villagers would drop off vegetables and melons that were too much for them to consume, and they would leave them on my table.

My living arrangements, however, remained an issue. Wherever the Mayor or I would ask, we were told that, had I been married with a family, they would have taken me in, but as a single man, no. Thus, I spent almost a month at the doctor's surgery. One day, I saw a recently built house which was uninhabited. When I asked about it, I was told that, while building it, the owner had become ill and passed away. His wife had worked as a tractor coupler. One day, the tractor overturned and the wife died beneath it. They had two children who were now living with an aunt near Samuil railway station. With the help of the Mayor of Samuil, I was able to rent a room in this empty house.

In the curriculum vitae I submitted for the job, I did not conceal anything about my life and my beliefs. The girl who accepted the documents began to read them. After a time reading, she burst into tears then came up to me and kissed me. She said that her father had also been through Belene. So, I now had my "own person" inside the administration.

The manager, as I have already mentioned, was also very well disposed to me. He said, "We are a new firm and we need specialists. It's as if you've fallen from the sky. So, I'll give you work but it will be off the books because you are prohibited. Go inside the plant and familiarize yourself with the production methods."

---

* These are traditional Middle-Eastern or Asian style, similar to the trouser part of **shalwar kameez**.

In the workshops, there were eight crews repairing wagons. There was also a workshop, for making and preparing spare parts. There was a fault inspector, where the axle shafts were checked for defects.

Five of the crew leaders were Turks and three were Bulgarian. The main engineer was Turkish as were many of the master technicians. About 80 per cent of the workers were Turks. The crane operators and the painters were all Turkish women. When the kitchen announced the day's menu on the board, they wrote "mutton with rice" or "mutton stew" and if the meat was pork they wrote "meat with rice" or "meat with potatoes" and so on. Many of the Turkish workers ate everything but some were quite conscientious about the meat they ate.

After almost two weeks of just wandering around the workshops, I told the instructor that I no longer felt comfortable walking around the plant without a job. Soon after, the manager called me into his office, and gave me a production quota manual, a fault register, and a notebook and pen. He told me I had to describe all the wagons that came into the plant, make a note of any damage or missing parts, and write down whatever repairs were needed; state whether this was a quick or medium-sized repair, or a general overhaul; and send the wagons on to the repair crew leaders, writing down the number of hours work to be allotted for the repair, according to the quota manual. There was to be no other work except that with a pen. As I was well acquainted with the structure of the wagons, the assignment was not difficult for me. I asked to be excused from the early morning meetings before work, as I could not stand the cigarette smoke. The foremen, technicians and bosses were all smokers and drinkers. Often they would drink secretly on the premises.

One day, one of the team leaders came up to me as I was examining the wagon they were about to repair and said, "Old Sando, you don't write enough."

"Aptrahim," I replied, "show me what I haven't written and I'll write it twice."

"No, you write everything right but the amount of money you write down is too low."

I told him I would see what I could do. So, I started noting down five or six hours extra, although I never wrote about any damage that was not really there. I just made the assessment larger. I handled the job just fine.

At one point, I ran into the Head of Payroll, who told me that I was writing down too many hours for the workers.

I said, "Come and show me which wagons I have written down but shouldn't have."

Because he only knew what wagons looked like when they were running on the rails, he said, "I'll catch you when you least expect it."

So, no one complained anymore; neither the workers, nor the bosses. And because the manager was not officially allowed to hire me as a fault checker, he told me that whenever the quota was over-fulfilled, he would reward me. And this he did.

Initially, I used my spare time on Saturdays and Sundays to read. Then, the village municipality gave me an allotment for growing melons. I picked up a hoe and went to check out the allotment. When I saw it, I sat down in the middle of it and ate my lunch. There were several people in each allotment around mine. It was the time of year to plant melons, watermelons, pumpkins, onions and beans. At some point, a trailer, towed by a tractor, arrived and unloaded half of its load of fertilizer in my allotment while the other half was taken off elsewhere. Some people planting a melon field nearby came and asked me in Turkish if I had any seeds. I said in Turkish that I did not. They not only gave me seeds but also helped me to plant them in the allotment. In this way, I became a gardener.

During my exile, I had a ten-day "leave" twice. On one of these occasions, I went to the hospital with severe arrhythmia and was put to bed. But as soon as my leave was over, Dr. Momchilova told me that she could not let me stay in hospital any longer, irrespective of my health condition.

I was prohibited from going anywhere but the village and the plant. I made friends with the Mayor, Ali Mollov, and he said to me, "Go wherever you please but let me know in advance, so I can cover for you." At first I doubted his honesty because, like all the village high-ups, he was a Party member. But over time, I became convinced of his loyalty. I started going into Razgrad when there was a good movie on or a play showing at the theatre. I would spend the night there, in the home of one of the workers. I also paid a few visits to some of my exiled comrades. Liuben was in Okrosh village, near Silistra, and Atanas was at Semerdzhievo village near Ruse. These visits were not discovered by the cops.

Two of the foremen at the plant were recruited to follow me, Yordan Koev-Chapraza (known as, 'The Buckle') and Ivan Gaidata ('The Bagpipe'). Koev and I became friends and one day he confessed that Captain Georgiev was his cousin and had ordered him to monitor what I said, where I went and whether any people came to see me. He also warned me that Ivan Gaidata would also be monitoring me. He regularly informed me if the Captain had paid a visit to his home and had asked about me. I handled Gaidata by talking only about work in his presence. Sometimes workers invited me to visit them at home, and occasionally I would take them up on their offer. Whenever there was a wedding or some other festivity in the village I was always invited.

For my entire stay at Huma, I was allowed only two breaks of ten days each, which I was permitted to spend with my family in Pernik. They visited me from time to time. They would stay with my Turkish neighbours with whom I was on excellent terms. Once, a larger group was visiting me and I asked a neighbour to lend me four chairs. So, after consulting with another neighbour, she brought me a packet of salt. I realized that she did not understand anything in Bulgarian, so I repeated it in Turkish and she then brought me four chairs. Another time, the store received some very nice apples. I asked Redzhib, the teacher, how to ask for two kilos of apples, but when I repeated the phrase to the saleswoman, she brought me a bra and asked me what size I wanted. Redzhib started laughing, so I gathered he had been teasing me.

As well as the school, the post office and the kindergarten, there was also a mosque in the village, though I wasn't interested in going there. I was warned to watch out for one person, even though he was also very friendly to me. Once, the Mayor, Ali Mollov, came up to me and said that Alito, the Post Office Chief, had bought a car in which he would be driving to Sofia on the Saturday morning, returning on Sunday night. So if I wanted to, I could go to Sofia with him and from there, go to Pernik and then come back with him the same way. I thanked him but declined his offer, explaining that if any of my Pernik neighbours were to see me, they would immediately call State Security on me.

I will describe an incident with Atanas Kisyov. He was allowed a ten-day leave, so he got on the train and when he reached the station in Sofia, two cops were waiting for him. They offered him a declaration to sign, and said that he should cooperate with them or he would not see his family again. Atanas asked them only if they knew the time of the return train. He did not get to see his family.

On 6th June 1977, I was released early, having spent three years and 12 days at the place of "internment". I was told that the exile law had been repealed. Liuben and Atanas were also released. At the militia office, Krum Bozhilov, the person who dealt with anarchists, told me, "Everyone's relatives came to ask for their release, only your wife didn't come once to ask for yours."

CHAPTER 11: ON THE TEMPERANCE
MOVEMENT IN BULGARIA

The Temperance movement in Bulgaria was founded before the First World War. As soon as the war was over, Temperance Societies were established at almost all the Houses of Culture in the country. The majority of the first Temperance activists were teachers. I know how, in my village, Kosacha, the teacher Vangelin Milanov signed up the elementary school students as members of the Temperance Society at the House of Culture. Not one of the village youths visited the pubs in those days. Many newspapers and journals on Temperance education were being published at the time, namely:

1. *Teetotaler*, from 1895 to 1925
2. *Sobriety*, from 1919, banned 1938
3. *Sober Struggle*, from 1932, banned June 1938
4. *Sober Thought*, from 1935, banned December 1938
5. *Zeal*, banned 1938
6. *Sober Society*, from 1927, banned 1938

Of the many Temperance Unions in existence at the time, the most active was the Youth Neutral Temperance Union (MNVS), founded in the city of Plovdiv in 1924. Subsequent congresses were held in Ruse, Stara Zagora, Pleven and Sofia in 1929, as well as in other cities.

In addition to the cultural and educational activities, there were endless arguments between anarchists and Communists. Up to 1934, the congresses had been relatively free. No one restricted the right to opinion, conviction and ideological affiliation. The Youth Neutral Temperance Union was founded on the principles of autonomy and independence. At one of the congresses in Gorna Oriahovitsa, Communists, anarchists and Tolstoyans were elected to the governing council. For years, the different currents within the Union cooperated. However, because of the different political persuasions of the membership, heated arguments sprung up on key issues. As early as their Fifth Congress in Yambol, the anarchists made the decision that "the anarchist, in order to be a true fighter, must give up alcohol."

In August 1931, the MNVS Congress was held in Veliko Turnovo. Anarchists and Communists openly brandished and crossed swords there. At the end, a new Governing Council was elected consisting of one Tolstoyan, one Communist, one Agrarian, one independent and three anarchists. A united front was built up, consisting of anarchists, Agrarians, Tolstoyans and independents. The reason this united front existed was because the Communists were slaves of sectarianism who viciously attacked anyone who disagreed with them.

The 8th Congress of the Union took place in August 1932 in Lovech. A new Governing Council was elected which consisted almost entirely of anarchists, with one Agrarian and one independent. At the 9th Congress in 1933, in the city of Svishtov, the Communists voted only with slogans. The elected Council consisted of seven anarchists, one Agrarian and one independent. After the coup of May 19 1934, the Union's legal activities were terminated. The work continued as outings to the mountains or in other covert forms.

The next one, the 10th Congress, was held in the autumn of 1934 in Plovdiv. In addition to the anarchists and independents, two members of the RMS (Workers' Youth Union) were elected at this Congress. The tendency towards confrontation between the different currents was overcome. The next Congress of the MNVS was held in Gabrovo on August 25–27 1935. At this Congress the Communists continued to vote with slogans.

An attempt was made to broaden representation, as far as this was possible. A leftwing socialist, a Communist, an Agrarian, and five anarchists were elected to the Council. Three of these were prohibited by the police from being on the Council. Runner-ups were elected in their place.

In August 1936, the 12th MNVS Congress was held in Stara Zagora. Two reports were presented, written by G. Sirakov and Toma Tomov. Five anarchists, four independents and one Agrarian were elected to the Governing Council. In the same year, the revolution in Spain began. About thirty anarchists, most of them teetotalers, left for Spain. Some of them never returned but were killed there and one was taken prisoner by Franco's troops. Relations within the Temperance Movement moved in an undesirable direction as Communists and anarchists constantly argued against each other. The MNVS Congress of 1937 in Gorna Oriahovitsa was to be the last one. In 1938, the Temperance Movement was disbanded. The monarcho-fascists were on the rampage, banning all legal activity. However, in the period after the Spanish Revolution, especially after the fascist-Bolshevik pact of 23rd August 1939, the Bolsheviks in our country sat on the sidelines, and the police persecuted only us.

I would like to mention the names of those anarchists active on the Temperance front: Dr. Ivan Balev, A. Sapundzhiev, Delcho Vasilev, Boris Rizov, Boris Mirkovenski, Georgi Popov, Bogdana Nacheva, Vasil Stavrev, Georgi Sirakov, Velko Zidarov, Nikolai Yovchev, Iliya Petkanov, Georgi Hadzhiev, Tania Vasileva, Hristo Kolev, Timofei Vodenicharov, Veneta Tsoneva, Stoyan Tsolov, Tzviatko Petkov, Nikola Mladenov, Radka Ruseva, Elisaveta Vasileva, Metodi Panchev and Toma Tomov. The last named did not have a good reputation among our comrades, although he was one of the best Temperance organizers.

After the coup on 19th May 1934, when all political parties and their newspapers were banned, Bolsheviks, anarchists, and others with leftist political beliefs, oriented their activities toward the Temperance newspapers, which were still being published. However, fights between different groups were endless. Occasionally, Temperance newspapers published information on the Spanish Revolution and on the

Part of the Stara Zagora Congress with participants of all ages on the left and the youth on the right.

rising tide of fascist and Nazi terror coming from the west. Consequently, the Bulgarian monarcho-fascists banned all Temperance newspapers in 1938.

While arguing endlessly with Todor Pepchev, Maksim Dimov and Spas Kirov, the RMS members in Pernik at the time, I defended the position that the state, regardless of its political colour, has been and will be a burden on the people. Their argument was that the state was bad because it was not in their hands, in other words, it was not in the hands of the Bolsheviks. We have seen, however, what happened when the state was entirely in their hands for over 45 years. There was no equality of the kind they had argued would emerge once power was in their hands. Eighty-six concentration camps dotted the country. The injustice and brutality of the new authorities had no parallel. All of their opponents were driven into these camps: anarchists, Agrarians, social democrats, Trotskyites; nationalists of all stripes: Legionnaires, Ratniks, Branniks[*], as well as former policemen, former officers, former ministers, disgruntled peasants, craftsmen, priests and Greek partisans from the defeated army of Markos.

Here I would like to illustrate my point with a quote from the wonderful memoirs of Radi Bonev, a Temperance activist from the time when the movement was at its peak:

"While working on my dissertation, I had the opportunity to become familiar with important Party archival materials and to obtain old records from past congresses of the All-Union Communist Party (Bolsheviks) and the Communist International. I began

[*] See note p. 52.

*to wade through it all, comparing what was reflected in the old
documents with the newer documents, and certain contradictions
jumped out. I observed carefully life in Moscow and in the whole
of the Soviet Union, that citadel of world socialism which saved
humanity from the brown Hitlerite plague; and I thought long
and hard about the destiny of our system. There was a marked
difference in remuneration between mental and physical labor. For
example, Professor Galkin received 8000 rubles, while our floor
cleaner received 80 rubles, a ratio of 1:100. One could not speak of
actual social justice, even less so of a "mature" or "developed" kind
of socialism – the invention of various "theoreticians". There were
expressions of typical bureaucratism in the Soviet administration.
We were given a poor impression by the extensive use of alcohol, a
negative attitude to the Jewish minority, and so on."*

Following the Bolshevik coup on 28th October 1945, we held
a nationwide Temperance Congress in Sofia. After an eight-
year ban, teetotalers gathered for our first "free" congress.

The surviving teetotalers in Pernik gathered in 1946 and re-
stored our activities as a Temperance Society. Among the first
founders were established teetotalers such as Kosta Hadzhiev,
Ivan Yordanov, Stoyan Milanov, Dimitur Vasilev, Laserman
Asenov, Liubomir Dzhermanov, Boyan 'The Granny' Aleksandrov, Boyan Aleksov, Spiro Nedialkov, Alexander Nakov,
Boris and Getso Serginovi, Bozhichko Hristov and others,
whose names I no longer remember. The Society's activities
rapidly expanded. Regular talks were organized on temperance themes. Concerts were held and in this way, we once
invited the famous singer Katia Popova†, whose performance
was so well-received by the audience that people in Pernik
talked about her for long after. Membership grew significantly
and the halls where we were allowed to gather were always

---

* From Bonev, R. (2004) **Conscience and Heart of a Man with no Alterna-
tive – Memoirs**. Veliko Tarnovo: Samizdat, pp 177-178 / Бонев, П. (2004),
Съвестта и сърцето човешко нямат алтернатива – Мемоари, Велико
Търново: Самиздат, стр. 177-178.

† 1924-1966, opera singer, soprano.

Death map of Bulgaria showing concentration camps and prisons.

packed. These halls were more often than not school rooms. We used the Ivan Rilski School most.

Towards the end of 1947, when it was no longer possible to conduct our anarchist activity legally, we all became members of the Temperance Society. At the general assembly in Pernik, I was elected Treasurer, while Liubomir I. Germanov was elected as Chair. When I was arrested on 6th December 1948, all the records of the Pernik Temperance Society were in my house: the cash-book, the register, the minute-book, the receipt book and savings-bank books in the name of the Society. When I returned home after five years in the Bolshevik camps, I went to look for these documents but my wife told me that in the spring of 1949, cops from State Security in Pernik were still collecting documents and had told her that the Temperance Society no longer existed.

In autumn 1956, Stoicho Trenev, at that time the Prosecutor in Pernik, came looking for me and asked me to help him re-establish the Temperance Society, only now under the new form of the "National Committee for Temperance". About thirty people gathered in the old court building. Dimitur Bretanov came from Sofia and after we had founded this National Committee for Temperance, no further activity was conducted. People had taken to drinking and no one was interested in temperance anymore.

Now, as I write my memoirs on the Temperance Movement, I have tried to look for any documents at the State Archives but discover that nothing on this movement was stored there. I had supposed that at least the documentation collected from my house would have been sent to the archive, but it seems as if the cops were only interested in the list of people with "sober thoughts". I am still unable to understand why the Bolsheviks destroyed the Temperance Movement, which played an important role in the development of our public and cultural life. It took shape as a rebellious and progressive social movement, yet it should not be understood merely as a cover for leftist ideas but, more than anything, as the necessity for working people to be sober and to fight for their liberation from all powerful oppressors, for the creation of a new world without slaves and masters.

Today we are witnessing an unprecedented growth in drug addiction, tobacco smoking, alcoholism and prostitution. The Bulgarian intelligentsia is not at all concerned about this condition of the younger generation. Intellectuals, too, are now slaves to power and money, which have corrupted doctors, teachers and all kinds of highly literate well-known personalities. The degradation is all encompassing.

Only the radical reorganization of society would get rid of these social ills.

CHAPTER 12: CHANGES

During this time, the so-called Cold War continued. Hungarians, Czechs and Poles tried to wrench themselves free from Big Brother's clutches. Only we, the Bulgarians, were good and loyal subjects of the evil empire. Upon my return from exile, I did not want to return to my old job at the Republic metal mine. Instead, I looked for a new job at the Central Enrichment Plant. When they heard I had extensive experience as a wagon inspector, they accepted me without any obstacles. I met my new managers, new workmates and new working conditions. The work itself was far safer than at the Republic mine.

I retired in September 1979. Almost all of my colleagues with whom I had worked came to visit me on the occasion of my retirement. They gave me a watch that I wear to this day. For more than a year after retirement, I did not work anywhere. But the pension, as is the case with all ordinary workers, was not enough. So I took on a job at the Lenin plant. This was the name of the steel plant at the time.

At that time, my partner, Kirilka, became ill. She had to have surgery to remove cancer of the colon. After another operation, when the malignant metastases appeared, she passed away on December 25 1982. I had lost my life partner, with whom we shared little happiness and much pain and suffering.

In 1982, joyful news came from Poland. Solidarity was gaining power and Lech Walesa became the mouthpiece of the Polish people's discontent with Big Brother's tutelage. Jaruzelski organized a pro-Soviet coup, but the Polish people had no intention of capitulating. Even before this, the Helsinki Accords* had been reached. Slogans such as "Communism with a human face" began to appear. After the Cuban crisis, it began to feel as if Bolshevik Russia was losing ground. Books

---

* These took place in 1975.

and brochures were being smuggled into our country, exposing Stalin's tyrannical regime. A guest of Dancho Damianov's brought in Karlo Stajner's book, in Esperanto, 7000 **Days in Siberia** – a book describing Stajner's visits to different sites in the Soviet Gulag. In Bulgaria, our own truth-dodger* was trying to contain the situation. In the Soviet Union, a host of senile geriatrics took turns after Stalin. When they saw that they were losing the race with the West, the powerful tried to figure out a way of preserving the regime. Gone was the tyrant's heavy fist. On November 10 1989, the noon radio broadcast announced that comrade Zhivkov had "renounced" his position of General Secretary of the Party. I was in the office of a state machine-building plant. Both the clerks and the management there greeted the news with joyful satisfaction.

I would like to take a moment to describe how the bosses used to build their villas around Rudartzi and elsewhere. Each day, our boss would set aside a few people from the work crews to build his villa. Their wages for the day were calculated at a lower rate than the work crews'. Whenever he needed timber, he would fill a truck with beams, joists and boards, while covering it under the camouflage of rotten boards from dismantled flooring. One day fire wood, another day reinforcing steel – there was always something being placed at the bottom of the truck and covered up with scrap iron sheets. So that was how it was. Workers stole whatever they could hide under their coat or in their bag, and the bosses looted by the truckload. Ours was one of many, and not the most brazen, not by a long shot. Most of the time, the militia looked the other way.

After the collapse of the great Soviet Union and the Warsaw Pact, after the Evil Empire no longer existed, with not a single gun fired in its defence, after the fall of the Berlin Wall, the world seemed to breathe a sigh of relief.

Here at home, the first course of action the Bulgarian

---

* A reference to Todor Zhivkov, Bulgarian Head of State from 1954 to 1989.

Communists took was to make sure they would not be held accountable for the atrocities they had committed against a section of the Bulgarian people. First, the dodgers such as Lukanov[*] split the old Bulgarian Communist Party into two "new" parties: the Bulgarian Socialist Party and the Union of Democratic Forces. They placed their loyal subjects in the UDF and gave them a bag of cash to publish the newspaper, **Democracy**. After the stablization of the two new parties, they called a "round table" where they accepted that there was guilt, but that there should be no blame. Zheliu Zhelev[†], as a Marxist student, became a proponent of the "velvet revolution". Not a single thug was punished.

After the disintegration of the Bolshevik order and the fake revolution of 10th November 1989, we, the survivors of the Bolshevik genocide of our movement in Southwest Bulgaria, immediately began to make connections with each other. Concerned about the future of the movement and our Federation, we began to organize meetings with our comrades from Pernik, Radomir, Dupnitza, Blagoevgrad, and Kiustendil. The focus of these meetings was to restore the local organizations, to recruit people suitable for organizing work and to establish links with comrades from other areas. In addition to establishing our organizations, we also had to think about club spaces. In Pernik, with the active help of the comrades Tzvetana and Liubomir Dzhermanovi, we were able to secure a clubhouse. Such clubs had already been created in Sofia, Blagoevgrad and Dupnitza. We searched for surviving literature to serve as our initial propaganda. We came into contact with comrades from all over the country. We began making arrangements for a national conference and the resurrection of the Federation. In this respect, the most active turned out to be our comrade from Kazanluk, Gancho Lazrov Damianov. He managed to organize comrades from the entire region.

---

[*] Lukanov was the last Prime Minister of Bolshevik Bulgaria, assassinated in 1996.

[†] The first post-Bolshevik President of Bulgaria.

After a preliminary meeting of prominent comrades who knew each other well, we decided to call a conference of comrades from around the country in order to rebuild the Federation. The meeting was scheduled for May 19–20 1990, in Kazanluk. The Kazanluk organization was second to none. They secured a hall, food and hotel accommodation for everyone.

The conference was attended by both elderly comrades and many young ones. The meeting was quite hearty. There was a somewhat initial debate between old and young about the name of the Federation. The old ones insisted on restoring the name, Federation of Anarchist Communists in Bulgaria, while the young ones asserted that the word "communist" had been defiled by those who had called themselves by this name, and it would therefore be more effective to simply use the name Federation of Anarchists in Bulgaria. Given these arguments from the young, their proposal was accepted.

Here is the Founding Document, approved by the conference:

Statement of the Founding Conference

Today, 19/05/1990, in Kazanluk, a founding conference of anarchist members took place to form the Federation of Anarchists in Bulgaria in order to bring together the regional anarchist groups and individual members according to a list that is an integral part of the current statement.

The Founding Conference was opened by Gancho Lazarov Damianov from Kazanluk, a key organizer and host of the conference. He addressed all present with the following words: "Dear friends, I am very happy to see so many like-minded people at this meeting. It should give us hope." Gancho Damianov suggested that a Chair and Secretary be elected to guide the meeting. The Founding Conference unanimously confirmed the composition of the conference

FAB Kazanlak Conference, 1990

facilitators. The Chair was Dr Liuben Yankulov and the Secretary was Sultana Stateva, both chosen unanimously.

Dr Liuben Yankulov took on the leadership of the conference and gave the floor to the eldest participant, 91-year old Angel Vulchanov, to greet the conference. With deep emotion the elderly Angel Vulchanov said:

"We have lived through dark and irresponsible times, when lie was truth, and truth was lie. The day has come for us to freely gather and freely express our ideas."

He wished success for the Founding Conference and its work, and invited all the participants to honour the memory of our lost and deceased comrades with a minute's silence.

Dr. Liuben Yankulov proposed the following agenda for the Founding Conference:

1. A report on the historical path of the anarchist movement in Bulgaria. Information on the European Anarchist Conference in Trieste from 17-20 April 1990, presented by Hristo Boichev.

2. Discussion and approval of the decision to establish the Federation of Anarchists in Bulgaria; report by Gancho

Lazarov Damianov.

3. Discussion and approval of the Statutes of the Federation of Anarchists in Bulgaria; report by Dr Liuben Yankulov.
4. Election of Federal Secretariat, Federal Secretary and Control Committee.
5. Election of Committee to update the movement's Platform.
6. Selection of a name for the newspaper and a name for the publishing house to be created – Konstantin Georgiev Ziapkov.

Following the agenda, the floor was given to Hristo Boichev, who read a report on the historical path of the anarchist movement in Bulgaria and on the European Conference of Anarchists, which took place in Trieste April 17– 20 1990.

Konstantin Kochinov, Boris Rizov, Dimitur Dimitrov, Trifon Terziiski and Stoyan Tsolov commented on the report and the information, approved the outcome of the conference and gave a positive assessment of the attendance at the conference.

On the second topic, Gancho Lazarov Damianov offered the proposal that the founding of the Federation of Anarchists in Bulgaria should be situated in Sofia in order for the movement to be better organized. He explained the justification for this. The participants supported the proposal and the conference decided to:

Establish the Federation of Anarchists in Bulgaria as a social movement, situated in Sofia, Triaditza Municipality, V. Dimitrov Street, Bl. 249.

A copy of the current decision to be given to the Federal Secretariat, to prepare an application to register the Federation at Sofia City Court, Corporate Division.

On the third item on the agenda, Dr Liuben Yankulov proposed the Draft Statutes of the Federation, which had previously been distributed to the participants in advance, and suggested moving on to a discussion of the document.

The following took part in the discussion: B. Rizov, Zh. Zheliazkov, K. Ziapkov, P. Popov, St. Tsolov, V. Momchev, Al. Nikov, S. Stateva, Dr. Pandiev, St. Stoinov, S. Pavlov, Bl. Ivanov, L. Yankulov. All the participants approved the Draft, offering certain amendments and additions, which were immediately recorded in the document.

Based on the document presented, a vote on the text was called for and the Founding Conference:

DECIDED:

To approve the Statutes of the Federation of Anarchists in Bulgaria in accordance with the text signed on each page by the Conference Chair, Dr Yankulov, and signed for approval by all participants, according to the attached list, which constitutes an inseparable part of the Statutes and the current statement.

A copy of the Statutes to be given to the Federal Secretariat, to attach to the Federation's application to Sofia City Court, Corporate Division.

On item 4 of the agenda, election of Federal Secretariat, Federal Secretary and a Control Committee, the Conference Chair suggested that the Secretariat consist of 9 members, and the Control Committee consist of 3 members. The proposal was put to the vote and was approved unanimously, after which the floor was given to the founding members to make nominations. After the ensuing discussion the following members were nominated to the Federal Secretariat:

1. Federal Secretary – Hristo Kolev Velinov from Karlovo

2. Members: Alexander Metodiev Nakov, Anastas Boyanov Mungov, Gancho Lazarov Damianov, Vanio Kolev Gurnev, Kostadin Georgiev Ziapkov, Liuben Ivanov Yankulov, Slaveiko Ivanov Pavlov, Trifon Todorov Terziiski.

The above-mentioned members were unanimously elected to the Federal Secretariat of the Federation, following an open vote with all in favour of the nominations.

To the Control Committee, following a discussion, the Founding Conference elected the following members: Dimitur Ivanov Stoev (Chair), Neno Atanasov Katsarski and Kostadin Iliev Zaharinov (members).

On item 5 of the agenda, after a discussion, a Commission, elected to update the movement's Platform, included the following members:

1. Slaveiko Pavlov
2. Stoyan Tsolov
3. Trifon Terziiski
4. Vesel Momchev
5. Gancho Damianov
6. Dr Liuben Yankulov
7. Zheliazko Petkov
8. Boris Rizov

On topic 6 of the agenda, the Founding Conference:

DECIDED:

To publish a newspaper titled *Free Thought* as the organ of the Federation. The book publishing house would be called "New World."

Before closing the Founding Conference, Dr L. Yankulov read the Draft Resolution of the Conference, which was put to the vote and unanimously approved by the Founding Conference. The written text of the resolution becomes an inseparable part of the current record. Having completed the agenda, the Founding Conference was closed at 18:30.

Secretary: Chair:
(S. Stateva) (L. Yankulov)

RESOLUTION

Approved at the National Conference of the FEDERATION OF ANARCHISTS IN BULGARIA, held on 19th and 20th May 1990, in the city of Kazanluk.

After 45 years of dictatorship the Federation of Anarchists in Bulgaria is alive. The physical and moral destruction of the freedom loving forces is not possible.

Our ultimate goal remains the same: to build a free society without a state and an economy without exploitation. Our basic principles remain unchanged: freedom, justice, morality. We consider mutual aid to be a fundamental natural and social law.

We are *bezvlastnitsi** because we are convinced that power, as well as the pursuit of power, corrupts.

We are socialists because we are on the side of freedom, equality and justice.

We prioritize collective ownership because it prevents exploitation and realizes technical progress in the interest of the collective without exploitation.

We will spread our ideas by legal and peaceful means. We reject violence in all its forms and directions. We fully disassociate ourselves from terrorism and we categorically condemn any attempts to be labelled as terrorists.

We make a realistic and sober assessment of contemporary conditions. We understand that a direct struggle for the realization of our ultimate goal is impossible without our participation in the struggle for a more democratic society. The hard road to freedom must be taken step by step, so we are in solidarity with all movements who seek greater freedom for the individual and an increase in the material welfare of all people.

With regards to the current struggle for the democratization of our society and the overcoming of the economic and political crisis, we stand for:

➤ the creation of a civil society in which freedoms are guaranteed by actual civil control, not only constitutionally.

➤ competition of ideas and beliefs, without right to a monopoly and without the right to forcefully impose ideas and beliefs on society.

➤ real freedom of speech and the press,

➤ the abolition of the death penalty, torture, and cruelty.

---

* Bulgarian word, synonymous with "anarchists" and meaning believers in the doctrine of no power.

➤ freedom of social forces to associate in organizations, movements, clubs, parties, and so on. We prefer the federative principle of organization.

➤ the right of working people to legally struggle to defend their material and intellectual interests, including the right to strike.

➤ municipal land ownership and the guaranteed right of the inhabitants to choose the forms of land management, but without sale and trade in land.

➤ the introduction of a tax system that limits state ownership and stimulates cooperative and private ownership as far as it excludes the possibility of exploitation.

➤ social policies that protect the disadvantaged, for continuous and just regulation of family incomes, for free education and medical services.

➤ public benefit funds raised from the confiscation of accumulated wealth of individuals or organizations in excess of a justly fixed limit.

➤ the maximum reduction of the bureaucratic apparatus

➤ the reduction of the length of the working day as a mechanism to deal with unemployment.

➤ the punishment within the law of those who commit moral and physical repression of others and for the punishment of the intellectual instigators of such acts. Even though we are one of the first and most cruelly repressed organizations, we stand against the escalation of revenge. Compensation for repression should come from the funds of the Bulgarian Communist Party and the Ministry of the Interior.

➤ the reduction of the military and the length of military service, moving towards their elimination within a united Europe.

➤ against any kind of religious or ethnic discrimination.

➤ for scientific education, free from party, political, class or religious influence.

> for an honest and appropriate environmental policy in accordance with contemporary science.

The conference elected:

Federal Secretariat

Commission to update the Platform of the organization

Liaison group for contact with other political organizations

Editorial Board

Spokesperson for the Federation

A newspaper to be published by the Federation, called **Free Thought**, with the publishing house known as **New World**.

Kazanluk, 20/05/1990

The newspaper came out, and also a magazine, *Free Society*. The idea for a publishing house was also realized and numerous books and brochures were published. I was a most active participant in all these activities. Then, the Federation organized two impressive congresses in Sofia. This time, comrades from the Union of Bulgarian Anarchists Abroad also attended. As I said earlier, before and during the pogrom against the movement in 1948, about 100 people managed to flee the country. Most of them settled in France, where they established a Union that began publishing a newspaper in Bulgarian, entitled *Our Road*. This newspaper traveled along invisible roads into Bulgaria. In France, too, the Union published over ten book titles in French and in Bulgarian.

Our organization in Pernik was re-established and began to work with the active involvement of Maria Vasileva, Boyan Aleksov, Laserman Asenov, Vladimir Petrov, Neno Katzarski, Stoyne Stoynev, Stamenko Dimitrov, Tzvetana and Liuben Dzhermanovi, Milcho Tsvetkov, Dimitur Stoev, Marin Metodiev, and myself, who, of course, is still here. Every Thursday, there were organizational and educational meetings. Everyone regularly attended the club and paid their membership dues.

I have been in contact with all the organizations in south-western Bulgaria: in Kiustendil, Dupnitsa, Blagoevgrad, Rado-mir, and many villages in those areas. I maintained close ties with the Varna anarchists, whom I frequently visited, but my age is now warning me to limit my travelling. Up until now I am still a member of the editorial board of the newspaper, *Free Thought*. I participate in the meetings of the organiza-tion in Sofia and Pernik. In my spare time, I often go to my native village, Kosacha, where I take care of 10 to 15 bee hives.

In 1999, I was allowed to read my file. I was given four folders with over 250 pages in each. Moreover, all of the documents in these files were dated prior to 1974. When I asked for my dossier after that year, I was shown a statement saying that my dossier from 1974 to the 1989 coup had been destroyed. The statement was signed by five people, members of some committee.

From what I have read, I realized that over the course of many years, every movement and action of mine had been accurately monitored. For this purpose, in addition to the official cops, a whole pack of informants, with code names, were used. Recalling the situations about which they wrote, I have been able to declassify almost all of them. I am doing this, not in order to seek profit or revenge, but to get a bet-ter understanding of the methods, motives and characters, of both the organizers as well as the informers. Neighbours, relatives, friends and children were used, which is the dirtiest thing, and it is unforgiveable.

I am finishing my notes. With them, maybe I have been able to answer the question, why I remained a committed anarchist up till now. I will return to the explanation with which I began. I will repeat some points in order to underline that the beginning and the end are inextricably linked.

Initially, I entered the movement somewhat spontan-eously and was possibly attracted by the eternally young

At the Anarchist Club in Sofia, Anton Nikolov and Stancho Karparob, September 2004

revolutionary romanticism at a time when the anarchists in Spain were the soul of the revolution. I was only 17 at the time! Later, however, I became interested in what the other political schools had to offer on the social question. The more I read and observed the events taking place in the world and my country, the more I was convinced in the correctness of the anarchist idea. No party offered real freedom and social equality. Hitlerism and Bolshevism, both premised on the priority of the defence of the working class, subsequently turned out to be the greatest oppressors of that working class. The "dictatorship of the proletariat" turned out to be a "dictatorship over the proletariat." Today, this rotten democracy is likely to bring back yet another dictatorship. In fact, we already have it: the dictatorship of the dollar.

Is anarchism the resistance of the free human being against any form of dictatorship? Is anarchism the defence of the idea of brotherhood, justice, mutual aid and human dignity? Yes, this is anarchism. That is why anarchism will always, even in our money-conscious times, have its followers. There will always be people ready to devote their strength, their time and their life to anarchism.

I did not set myself the task of describing my life in detail but, primarily, those aspects of it related to my anarchist activity; which I have no intention of interrupting yet.

– Alexander Nakov

With his first great-grandson Ivo in the Dubova mahala neighborhood, May 1990.

Appendix I: WHY THE MOVEMENT NEEDS ORGANIZATION[*]

BY ALEXANDER NAKOV

Now, it is more than a century since, in the hideous face of the bourgeoisie, Proudhon cast his famous charge. Namely, property is theft. In doing this, he signed the birth certificate of social anarchism.

To clarify, what is social anarchism and why is it necessary to make some distinctions to define the term more clearly?

Anarchism, as the negation of authority, oppression and the enslavement of man is a natural human predisposition that is as old as humanity itself. People have risen up, both individually and collectively, against all forms of oppression, regardless of whether it was in the family, or whether it was social, political or religious. This anarchism has always been expressed through struggle, in a pure and wild rebellion, and its roots are deeply embedded in instinct rather than reason.

But anarchism as a doctrine which aims to establish a new order, expressed in a concrete attempt to transform social structures and change the relations between members of society – this anarchism comes from the last [19th] century.

Anarchism, after a centuries-long incubation period, obtained its scientific grounding in the works of talented thinkers, who did not sanitize the original, but gave it an articulated form. They created a social ideology that was able to present an answer to many questions by pure analysis.

Now, more than a century old, anarchism has its past, a past that is concurrently filled with glory and dreams. It is glorious because of the richness of its ideas that reach thinking, progressive students and workers, who will eventually be able to realize them. It is also glorious because of the passion it has given to all the people who have engaged

---

[*]The original of this text first appeared in the FAB paper, *Free Thought*. The translator is unknown.

with it, by writing, speaking out and acting. Despite the many tragedies, with some paying with their lives, these ideas have been able to survive. From Tokyo to Barcelona, Chicago to Moscow and London to Rome, the anarchists' brave struggle has contributed to human emancipation.

The past is also dreamed about because, despite its simple, logical and rational ideology; despite the almost religious belief, that has driven its heroes to the gallows, in a world where they showed the courage of those who know how to die for an honourable cause and were ready to sacrifice themselves for it; despite all that, anarchism has not succeeded and become a reality in any country.

The explanations for this are many, but insufficient. To this day, there are still people who tend to see in anarchism only negation. Negation has its place only up to the point in which it is a prelude to creation. The contribution of those thinkers and propagandists, who in the last century made anarchism social, brought it beyond self-negation and made it the creative face of the revolution. Unfortunately, plenty of anarchists were unable or did not want to learn this lesson.

I still believe that only when anarchists are organized in a consistent, serious and united manner, will they finally be able to reach out and filter across the world scene, cease being passive witnesses, and instead will become active participants in the human purpose to create each day.

As I have already mentioned, anarchism has not been able to realize itself. The attempt in Spain was an exception. Spain is also a great historical experience to which we are obliged to constantly turn and reflect upon.

On Organization

In our social circles, we can honestly agree that organizational problems have generated the liveliest arguments. This, I believe, is because of the fact that there are two completely different modes in understanding anarchism and we need to define them both if we are to cast light upon the problem. This is because it is clear that the anarchist who claims to belong to a certain philosophical school does not necessarily need organization. Specifically, that person is an individualist. In contrast, the revolutionary anarchist, since he aims to transform society, even now believes it is necessary to create a solid structured organization that is able to provide all its members with close connections and continuous mutual aid.

In order to achieve this, he is required to voluntarily limit a part of one's freedom and subject himself to a certain discipline, freely accepted, and only when it is immediately necessary, so that the common task is the ability to be effective and cohesive.

In short, there are two choices for those who claim to belong to anarchism. On the one hand, anarchism can be considered as an element of the social condition, an element that brings its own proof that does not give rise to a need for organization. Such a choice reaches out in the framework of purely individual activity. On the other hand, anarchism is considered a social doctrine that can be immediately realized. This also needs collective action and determination in order to be realized, and this requires stable organization. This choice is necessary, because groups of people have a valuable right to existence only if those people are able to respond to the basis and the aims of such a social grouping. If not, a kingdom of confusion and a lack of will is created.

From this perspective we could argue that the only ones who can form an organization are the ones who accept its principles and the necessary discipline required by the organization. The only possible members of such an anarchist revolutionary organization are those who accept that such a transformation is viable in the times we are currently living in.

All in all, we organize because it is necessary that we act now, organizing with the aim of social transformation and the necessary means of social reconstruction.

Organization is also necessary because each movement needs an organized structure: anarchist, because the aim is the construction of a free society; revolutionary, because this is the way to create a fundamental shift in the established social order.

What I am saying is that we should aim to accurately limit and define the organizational problem that exists in our circles. The goal that anarchists are struggling to achieve, the creation of a society of free people, cannot be achieved by methods that negate the ends.

– Alexander Nakov, 2011

Alexander Nakov at the FAB Centre, Sofia, March 2012.

Appendix II: PLATFORM OF THE FEDERATION OF ANARCHIST COMMUNISTS IN BULGARIA, 1945*

Basic positions

We reject the present social system of State and capitalist centralization, as it is founded on the principle of the State which is contrary to the initiative and freedom of the people. Every form of power involves economic, political or spiritual privilege. Its application on an economic level is represented by private property, on a political level by the State and on a spiritual level by religion. These three forms of power are linked. If you touch one, the others are changed and, inversely, if you keep one form of power, it will inevitably lead to the re-establishment of the other two. This is why we repudiate the very principle of power.

We are supporters of the abolition of private property, of the State, and of religion, and of the total suppression of every form and institution of constraint and violence. We reject every teaching and every social, political and eco-nomic-political movement aimed at maintaining the State, private property, the church, and constraint and violence in social relations.

We repudiate fascism, which is a historic attempt to re-store absolutism, autocracy, and the strength of the political form of power with the aim of defending the economic and spiritual dominance of the privileged classes.

We reject political democracy, as it does not foresee the disappearance of the principle of power, and drives the masses to bewilderment by leading them, through lies and illusions, into fights which are against their interests, and corrupts them through the exercise of power and the main-taining of the appetite for domination. Political democracy,

* Translated by Nestor McNab from a text at **www.fondation-besnard.org**. Used with permission from the website **anarkismo.net**.

furthermore, shows that it is totally incapable of solving the great social problems and that it fosters chaos, contradictions and crime as a result of its social foundations based on the centralized State and capitalism.

We repudiate State socialism as it leads to State capitalism – the most monstrous form of economic exploitation and oppression, and of total domination of social and individual freedom.

We are for anarchist communism or free communism, which will replace private property with the complete socialization of lands, factories, and mines, and of all goods and instruments of production. The State will be replaced by a federation of free communes regionally, provincially, nationally, and internationally united. The church and religion will be replaced by a free individual moral and a scientific vision.

Unlike all other socio-economic and political concepts and organizations, Anarchist Communism is federalist.

The new social organization that will replace the State will be built and run from the bottom upwards. All the inhabitants of any given village will form the local free commune, and all the local free communes will unite regionally, provincially, nationally, and internationally in unions and federations and in a universal general social confederation.

The new organization of society's production will be formed by a tight network of countless local agricultural enterprises, artisans, mines, industry, transport, etc., united on a regional, provincial, national, and international level in production unions and federations as part of a general confederation of production.

Society's new organization of exchange, consumption and supply will likewise be represented by a dense and complex network of regional, provincial, and national organizations, unions and federations, grouped in a general confederation of exchange and consumption for satisfying the needs of all inhabitants.

All human social activity and all transport, communications, education, healthcare, and so on, will be organized in a similar fashion.

With this organizational system of all the functions of the various aspects of social life, there will be no place in society for the power of one individual over another or for the exploitation of one by another.

The basic principle of production and distribution for the building of the new social system will be: everyone will produce according to their possibilities and everyone will receive according to their needs.

Tactics

The realization of this social ideal of equality, solidarity and freedom can only be brought about by the united workers and peasant masses, inspired by anarchist communism and organized into ideological, professional, exchange and consumption, cultural, and educational groups.

Anarchist communism, while repudiating the State, rejects the involvement of the workers in the administration bodies and institutions of the State, in the parliament, and in any vote for the official management of the State.

As the sole means of efficient struggle, as a defence of the immediate interests of the working masses, and for the realization of the full ideal of humanity's freedom, anarchism recognizes only the direct action of the workers themselves, initiated by their economic organizations and expressed through strikes, sabotage, boycotts, general strikes, insurrections, and the social revolution. In consequence, anarchism rejects all forms of organization and struggle by political parties, considering them sterile and ineffective, unable to respond to the goals and the immediate tasks and to the interests of the workers in the towns and villages. The true strength of the workers is in the economy and their economic organizations. Only there lies the terrain where capitalism can be undermined. Only there lies the true class struggle.

Organization

The radical social re-organization demanded by anarchist communism requires the organizational action of all the forces on whom this historical task is incumbent.

It is above all necessary for the partisans of anarchist communism to be organized in an anarchist communist ideological organization.

The tasks of these organizations are:

➢ to develop, realize and spread anarchist communist ideas;

➢ to study all the vital present-day questions affecting the daily lives of the working masses and the problems of the social reconstruction;

➢ the multifaceted struggle for the defence of our social ideal and the cause of working people;

➢ to participate in the creation of groups of workers on the level of production, profession, exchange and consumption, culture and education, and all other organizations that can be useful in the preparation for the social reconstruction;

➢ armed participation in every revolutionary insurrection;

➢ the preparation for and organization of these events;

➢ the use of every means which can bring about the social revolution.

Anarchist communist ideological organizations are absolutely indispensable in the full realization of anarchist communism both before the revolution and after.

These organizations are formed on a local level. Every local organization chooses a secretary, whose task is to keep in contact with other similar organizations. The secretaries of all the organizations of one locality with a certain number of inhabitants constitute the general organization of the locality. All the local organizations unite, by region and province, in regional and provincial unions. Contact between the unions is assured by the respective secretaries. All the provincial unions of the country are united in the Federation of Anarchist Communists in Bulgaria. Activities are coordinated by the Federal Secretariat. The members of each secretariat form part of the local organization in their area of residence, and it is obligatory for every initiative of theirs to pass through the local organization, and therefore be considered an initiative of the latter. The secretariats are merely liaison and executive bodies with no power.

Only anarchist communists can be members of the anarchist communist ideological organizations.

A second type of organization is the workers' syndicate, also based on the federative principle, organized by workplace or by trade, and united into production or trade unions in a general federation of workers' syndicates.

These organizations, created with the participation of anarchist communists, adopt the tactic of direct action and reject the struggles of political parties and all interference by political parties in the workers' organizations. Their tasks are:

> ➤ the defence of the immediate interests of the working class;
> ➤ the struggle to improve the work conditions of the workers;
> ➤ the study of the problems of production;
> ➤ the control of production, and the ideological, technical and organizational preparation of a radical social reconstruction, in which they will have to ensure the continuation of industrial output.

All workers who accept their structure, tactics and tasks may be members of these organizations.

When conditions do not permit the existence of such organizations, anarchist communist workers join other independent syndicalist workers' organizations, while defending their concept of direct action and their anti-party position. The ORPS* would appear to be such an organization today.

A third type of organization must group the peasantry. This is the locally-created agricultural labour organization, united on a regional, provincial and national level in a general federation which, together with the federation of workers' syndicates, make up the national confederation of labour.

The tasks of these agricultural labour organizations are:

> to defend the interests of the landless peasants, those with little land and those with small parcels of land;
> to organize agricultural production groups, to study the problems of agricultural production;
> to prepare for the future social reconstruction, in which they will be the pioneers of the re-organization and the agricultural production, with the aim of ensuring the subsistence of the entire population.

The agricultural labour organizations are built on the basis of sector and reject all struggles by political parties and their interference in the organizations. They apply the tactic of direct action, whenever possible, in their specific conditions, including refusing to pay taxes, boycotting the State, production strikes, etc.

The members of these organizations can be landless peasants, those with little land, and those with small parcels of land, who work the land themselves without the use of wage labour.

When the conditions to create such organizations do not exist, anarchist communist peasants join other similar labour

---

* The **Obsht Rabotnischeski Profesionalen Sayuz**, or General Workers Trade Union, was formally founded in March 1945 and was dominated by the Bulgarian Communist Party. It became the Central Council of Trade Unions in 1951 and the Central Council of Bulgarian Trade Unions in 1972 before merging into the Confederation of Independent Trade Unions of Bulgaria in 1990.

organizations, with the aim of promoting within them their vision of direct action and struggle against political parties and the tactic of peasant direct action. The OZPS* could be considered such an organization.

A fourth type of organization is the cooperative. Anarchist communists participate in all types of cooperative, bringing to them the spirit of solidarity and of mutual aid against the spirit of the party and bureaucracy. Agricultural production cooperatives today merit special attention, as they will become more important and will play a decisive educational role in the future construction of an anarchist communist social system.

Another type of organization are those of young people, women, temperance groups, Esperantists and other cultural organizations whose members support the ideas and the struggles of the anarchist communist ideological and economic organizations of the working people.

Relations between the aforementioned organizations are on a functional basis that recognizes the full freedom and independence of the members and the organizations, and excludes all external interference and all subordination of one organization to another. The reciprocal dependence between the various types of organization can only be based on their ideological commonality and unity, the common goal to which they all aspire.

Organizational decisions within anarchist communists' organizations are made unanimously, and not by majority. The decision of the majority is not binding on the minority; persuasion should always be sought. In practice, the minority generally rallies to the decision of the majority, which reserves the right to express the correctness of its position, once it has been demonstrated in fact. Thanks to this principle, which is widely applied within the anarchist movement, splits, enmities, and arguments are rare.

* The **Obsht Zemedelski Profesionalen Sayuz**, or General Peasants' Trade Union (OZPS) was set up as an independent syndicalist union. However, it too fell under Communist Party control and dissolved in 1951.

However, within the mass economic organizations and the other organizations, decisions are taken by majority vote and are binding, as only in this way can unity be achieved, unity that is absolutely indispensable in mass organizations. But in certain cases where there is profound disagreement, the minority may be freed from the obligation to apply a general decision, on condition that it does not prevent the execution of such a decision.

All the aforementioned organizations share the common task of preparing the radical social reconstruction throughout the country. During the social revolution, they will each carry out (within their own domain) the expropriation and socialization of the means of production and of all goods.

Immediate tasks

At present, the Federation of Anarchist Communists in Bulgaria has adopted the following slogans:

The creation of free worker and peasant local councils and committees elected directly and not as representatives of political parties, organized and controlled by the people. These councils and committees must take completely in hand, or control, the political direction of the country.

The role of these councils and committees is to express the wishes of the working masses and of coordinating the efforts of all in order to construct a complete social system and ensure its functioning. They are united on local, regional and national levels and represent the whole people's political force, thought and will.

The adoption by Bulgarian workers and peasants of the International Workers' Association, to defend the worldwide interests of all working people and impede any forthcoming war.

The clear and categorical rejection of all forms of class collaboration.

Recognition of the right of workers to struggle freely to

defend their material interests, to improve their conditions and to strike.

Workers' control of production and a share of the benefits.

The reduction of wage differences between the various categories of civil servants, State workers and private sector workers, tending towards the introduction of a family wage.

Exemption from all taxes for workers, low-level employees, small peasants and all low-paid levels of society.

Free and voluntary agricultural cooperative associations.

Free and voluntary cooperation between small artisan enterprises.

Progression towards a complete cooperative system of exchange, food supply and consumption, and towards cooperative development to include domestic and foreign trade and social security.

Increases in the prices of agricultural production up to an average level and a reduction to the same level of the prices of industrial products, based on real retail prices and a just and egalitarian remuneration for labour in the towns and countryside.

Organization of the struggle against speculation and the black market by the labour associations, producers' associations, exchange and consumption associations and by the public naming of all speculators and traffickers.

The creation and development of regular, high-quality commercial relations throughout the country, with the rapid satisfaction of needs with regard to basic essentials, such as clothing and footwear, through foreign imports.

The financial stabilization of the country with a streamlining of the bureaucratic apparatus, with a real (not provisional) State budget and economy, with the complete elimination of all unnecessary spending (such as the costs of war), and with a real increase (not just a demagogic one) in the national production.

Complete freedom of speech, of the press and of organization and assembly for all non-fascists. The suppression of all State and police control – left over from the fascist period – of cooperatives, trade unions and other organizations. The government must fulfil its promises in this regard.

Opposition to all dictatorships of whatever name or colour.

Suppression of the death penalty and of all special laws.

The disappearance of all concentration and labour camps or workhouses with the aim of punishing; dissolution of the forced labour system, applied as a police method.

Struggle against the remnants of fascism and vigilance against all activity against the people, under the aegis of the various labour, production and ideological organizations of the workers and peasants.

The grouping of all worker and democratic elements into egalitarian, militant unions in order to resist strongly and effectively the growing reaction.

War reparations to be made by war criminals.

The dissolving of the army and the suppression of obligatory military service and the militaristic education of young people both inside and outside schools.

The creation of a voluntary popular militia (not controlled by any party), recruitment to which will be solely effected from among the workers and peasants, and controlled by the worker-peasant organizations.

Fully scientific teaching and education, free of all political party and class influence, widely available to the new generations.

Free, widely available healthcare for everyone.

The total exclusion of all religious interference from teaching and the family.

Aid to the population under the control of the labour, production and ideological organizations of the workers and peasants.

Bread, freedom, peace and jobs for all workers and the progressive layers of the Bulgarian people.

Long live the international solidarity of the workers!
Long live anarchist communism!

Kiustendil, Aleksander Nakov at the anarchist Todor
Angelov's memorial in the city of Kiustendil, 1988.

Appendix III: LETTER CONCERNING A RELATIVELY UNKNOWN MOVEMENT*

From Alexander Nakov to Rob Blow
26 October 2013, Pernik

Dear Rob,

I received your postcard/letter not too long ago. Thank you! In connection with my booklet/dossier, I understand that you are now working again on editing the translation.

From what Mariya tells me, I understand that you have said that the Bulgarian anarchist movement isn't very well known. It's true, we don't have Sacco and Vanzetti, Louise Michel or Durruti. Neither do we have events such as the Chicago Martyrs, Kronstadt, the Makhnovists, the Paris Commune and the Spanish Revolution. But we do have Hristo Botev, Georgi Sheytanov, Vasil Ikonomov and the heroes of Yambol[†], of which 26 were executed by firing squad in 1923.

Our newspaper, *Free Thought* (Svobodna Misyl), was founded in 1920, before Errico Malatesta's *Umanità Nova*[‡].

Bulgarian anarchists founded their organization, the Federation of Anarchist Communists in Bulgaria (FACB). These Bulgarian anarchists were cruelly persecuted by every regime, whether installed by democrats, fascists or Bolsheviks. Our movement gave them plenty of victims. Those who were the cruellest against us were the so-called Communists. When they installed themselves in Bulgaria, their first task was to or-

---

* That is, relatively unknown outside of the Balkans; translated from Esperanto by the editor.

[†] Hristo Botev (1848-1876), poet and revolutionary; Georgi Sheytanov (1896-1925) and Vasil Ikonomov (1898-1925), anarchists and proponents of direct action; the heroes of Yambol: 26 anarchists arrested without trial March 26-27 1923 and executed in the barracks of the 4th Cavalry Regiment by order of Konstantin Mouraviev, Minister for War.

[‡] *Umanità Nova*, also first published in 1920; now the journal of the Italian Anarchist Federation (FAI).

ganize enough concentration camps and prisons. First of all, they put us into these prisons. Around 600 of us were placed in concentration camps. Most were killed there. Around 100 managed to flee abroad, with most of those based in Paris. From there, they organized themselves in the Bulgarian Libertarian Union in exile (ULB) and began to publish the paper *Our Road*.

I am starting to see only dimly and I can't walk very well. From time to time I lose my balance. Such is old age.

In friendship,
Alexander

Commemorating the anniversary of the murder of Vasil Ikonomov in the village of Belitsa

Appendix IV: THE BULGARIAN ANARCHIST MOVEMENT IN 2013

BY ROB BLOW & MARIYA RADEVA[*]

After the Bolshevik's 45-year attempt to obliterate the Federation of Anarchist Communists (FAB) in Bulgaria, along with other libertarian organizations, the Bulgarian anarchist scene is a shadow of the mass movement it once was. Since 1990, the natural passage of time has also meant that most of the movement's old guard are now no longer with us. However, a new generation of anarchists has begun to come of age, disillusioned by the Bolshevik project but nevertheless unwilling to go along with the prospect of the neoliberal capitalist alternative to state socialism/state capitalism.Some of these women and men gathered around FAB during the 1990s and after, while others formed initiatives independent of, and sometimes in sharp disagreement with, the re-established Federation.

What follows is a modest review of the anarchist scene in Bulgaria today, mainly focusing on the capital, Sofia. It is our intention to show the various organizational forms which anarchists have been putting into practice in recent years.

The necessity of anarchist organization that Alexander Nakov argues for in his address to the reader looms large wherever anarchists challenge the existing social order. Yet in those societies which experienced Bolshevik rule, where vanguardism and authoritarianism came to encompass the entirety of so-called "communist" tactics, ideas and practice in the popular imagination, anarchist communist organizing is particularly challenging.

*   *   *   *   *

---

[*] Based on comments by Todor Ivanov, Zlatko Kostadinov, Lyuben Barzakov, Petar Piperkov, Samuel Yosifov, Evgenii Nikitin, Veselin Nikolov and others.

The Federation of Anarchists in Bulgaria (FAB)

The endeavours of those anarchists who survived years of the Bolshevik Gulag helped to kick-start the FAB, together with the new, younger comrades who have come along since 1990. The word "communist" was dropped from the Federation's name at this time, a decision that, with hindsight, some have come to regret. Many of the anarchists in the early post-Bolshevik years emerged from the punk scene at the time. However, this was not the only path that led people to adopt anarchist views. Many turned to anarchism in response to personal experiences of the state socialist school system, of free-market capitalist workplaces, or because of feelings of impoverishment and social isolation.

At a critical moment, the FAB provided a much needed political education to those who, in one way or another, came into contact with the Federation. In 2003, an informal group known as the Anarchist Popular Resistance Front (APRF) was formed within FAB, becoming its most active element at the time. The APRF maintained a website, published leaflets and was involved in various direct actions. The group was renamed 'Vasil Ikonomov'* in 2005, publishing *A Program for Radical Transformations in Bulgaria* and the newsletter *Anarchist*. The FAB, however, did not increase in size and the aging old guard has not been replenished. At the same time, many of the youth left to start up or join other initiatives. However, few of those initiatives are explicitly anarchist today.

People left the FAB for a variety of reasons, such as generational or tactical disagreements. There were differences over how to respond to contemporary fascism and antisemitism; and the desire to focus more on anti-racism, migrant rights, the emancipation of women and animal rights.

Today, the FAB appears to be an ideological organization

---

* Named after the famous Bulgarian anarchist Vasil Bonchev Ikonomov, 1899-1925.

engaged in the analysis of
revolutionary politics and
anarchist propaganda, which
it does primarily through its
paper, *Svobodna Misyl* (Free
Thought). For those who have
remained in the FAB, it is a
method of mobilizing those
who are ready and willing to
participate in a united social
struggle. In terms of creating
propaganda, finance is always
an issue and the the organization's meagre financial
resources do not allow the

March 2012, FAB's centre, Sofia.
Aleksander Nakov, Mariya Radeva

FAB to do as much as its members would like. The paper is
funded primarily by contributions from anarchists in exile,
who, one after another, are now passing away. The anarchist
movement as a whole does not possess the means to produce
its own propaganda at any substantial scale so printing is
done on costly commercial presses. Consequently, the future
of the paper, *Svobodna Misyl*, as the FAB's main organizing
tool, remains uncertain.

The Wider Anarchist Scene

The FAB is not alone on the Bulgarian anarchist scene
today. Anarchist Resistance (AR) was the other main group
to have emerged in Sofia at the turn of the 21st century. Unlike
the FAB, AR attracted a markedly younger pool of anarchists.
There was some flow of membership between these groups
in the first years, around the time when the groups collab-
orated on publishing *Svobodna Misyl* and the news-sheet,
AnarhoSyprotiva (Anarcho-Resistance), which appeared
as an insert. A key distinction between the two currents
is that the FAB might be seen more or less as a "classical"

social anarchist grouping, particularly focusing on class war and class struggle (arguably to the neglect of other aspects of oppression and struggles for emancipation). AR, on the other hand, pays more attention to LGBTQ rights, feminism, various environmental causes, animal liberation, and veganism. Other ideas similar to those held by groups such as CrimethInc in the West are incorporated into AR's conception of class struggle. One ongoing disagreement between both currents is that around Sofia Pride, in which elements within the FAB have been critical of the tendency towards what they see as identity politics. Members of AR also participated in the creation of Indymedia Bulgaria, the "Life After Capitalism" project, Anares Books, and the Bulgarian Social Forum. Some more recent initiatives and writers collectives such as "Left Thoughts for Rightist Days" claim to have been strongly influenced by AR in their ideas and practices.

Social Centres and Syndicalist Groups

The first social centre in Sofia, Xaspel, was set up in 2010 by AR people and others, and was dedicated to environmentalism and egalitarianism. The rent for the centre was subsidised by an environmentalist NGO called Za Zemiata (For the Earth). However, over time, the centre's membership and orientation shifted with many anarchists eventually leaving the collective. Xaspel attracted the attention of the Rosa Luxemburg Stiftung[*], enabling them to run political educational programmes and produce public commentaries for an international audience. The group, now known as Xaspel Social Centre/New Left Perspectives, does not identify itself as anarchist.

Soon after, a second social centre, Adelante, funded by the FAB in its early period, was set up. Before long, the collective parted from the FAB and later distanced itself from anarchist or other ideological labels. Adelante today is a lively place

[*] Based in Germany, a research foundation connected to Die Linke, the Left Party.

for educational, social and cultural events in the spirit of autonomism. For a number of years the collective has spread the ideas and practices of direct democracy and popular assemblies. During the anti-government protests in Sofia in the summer of 2013, a general assembly gathered every night at the Orlov Most* bridge.

One initiative that strives to combine social, cultural, educational, workplace organization and community work is the Mutual Aid Cooperative. Set up in 2012, the collective includes both libertarian communists vanguardist leftists, among others, who all share the rent and expenses. The cooperative steers clear of anti-communism, sectional group commitments, paid NGO activism and charitable foundations. The Mutual Aid Cooperative hosts a number of independent initiatives such as the anti-tuition student organization, Priziv za Obrazovanie (Call for Education), a workplace struggle group, Rabotnicheski Glas (Workers' Voice), the Civil Initiative for Public and Rail Transport† and a tutoring program for impoverished inner-city youth. The cooperative's activists see grassroots educational initiatives as a way toward a community-based struggle against the everyday effects of institutionalised racism, for example, early school drop-out rates for the Roma.

A syndicalist group known as the Autonomous Workers Union (AWU) was established by former members of FAB in 2010, organizing its first protest in front of the Bulgarian Industrial Chamber on 1st May 2012. It has sections in several cities in Bulgaria, although not all members are anarchists. The AWU rejects the triple axis of the state, the capitalist class and conventional trade unions. Its main focus today is in expanding the AWU nationally, building regional and trans-national alliances, and popularising the ideas and tactics of anarcho-syndicalism. Similar to all other groups in Bulgaria,

---

* **Orlov Most**, Eagle Bridge

† Grazhdanska initsiativa za obshtestven i relsov transport

the AWU struggles to rent space for their union and raise funds to produce propaganda. The AWU previously started up an agricultural producer consumer cooperative which, at the time of writing, has entered its second agricultural cycle.

At the monument to V. Ikonomov, the anarchists H. Kolev, N. Arshinkov, C.K. Velinov and T. Katarov.

Most recently, a social center was set up in Varna. Based on direct democratic principles, Varna Solidarity Centre was formed in March 2013 during the mass protests against the energy distribution monopolists. The collective participates in initiatives that demonstrate direct democracy and political and economic alternatives to capitalism. Its members organized general assemblies during the protests in Varna and set up a service cooperative with free markets and hosted screenings, lectures, classes and festivals on various anti-authoritarian and anti-capitalist themes, including workplace occupations. Varna Solidarity Centre also offers space to a section of the Autonomous Workers Union.

Anti-Racism, Feminism and Pacifism

There are also those anarchists who are, or have been, involved with some of the already mentioned initiatives and collectives, yet who question or reject what they view as the patriarchal overtones and class reductionism of anarchist (and communist) revolutionaries. Such anarchists can be found in various mixed groups that protest against or fight everyday instances of violence against people of colour, women and LGBTQ people. Examples of these groups are: the No Border Network, which is dedicated to supporting undocumented migrants detained in Bulgaria; Anti-Lukov which offers resistance to the institutionally tolerated neo-Nazi Lukov march*; and the now defunct XoPa (People against Racism) group.

Overview

Overall, the anarchist movement in Bulgaria has a long way to go before it can regain anything close to its former mass character, but it is certainly not alone in this respect. What exists now is very much a mixed bag, a vibrant if disjointed political scene. However, for a movement that was utterly buried by Stalinism not so long ago, then swamped with neoliberal propaganda, it is doing reasonably well to persist as much as it does. Its future, its ability to gain strength and stability, depends very much on what resources and discipline anarchists can muster for collective action toward shared goals. This is the example that Alexander Nakov has set for us all.

Links†

Svobodna Misyl (Free Thought):	http://sm.a-bg.net/
Autonomous Workers Union:	http://arsindikat.org/
Priziv for Education:	http://priziv.org/
Workers' Voice:	http://rabglas.blogspot.com/
Leftist Thoughts for Rightist Days:	http://levimisli.wordpress.com/
Life after Capitalism:	www.lifeaftercapitalism.info/

---

* A march to commemorate the early 20th century Nazi, General Hristo Lukov.

† Links as of February 2014

No Borders BG:	http://noborderbulgaria.word-press.com/
AntiLukov:	http://antinazimarch.blogspot.com/
Haspel:	http://xaspel.net/
New Left Perspectives:	http://novilevi.org/
Varna:	www.facebook.com/solidaren-centyrvarna
	http://varnacoop.com
Za Zemiata:	www.zazemiata.org/

Appendix V: BACKGROUND TO THE ENGLISH LANGUAGE EDITION

BY VIOLA M. ANDO

I met Alexander Nakov at the SAT Esperanto Congress in Belgrade, 2006. For those not familiar with the international Esperanto movement, SAT is the left-wing, progressive World Non-national Association, in which there exists a sizable anarchist grouping known as the Libertarian Fraction.

One day, Alexander handed me a copy of his book saying, "I want you to read it." Now, as I speak Japanese, Esperanto and English, I was not sure why he had given me a book in Bulgarian. Nor do I know how many copies he had with him or who else he had given his book to.

He told me that he had once met another Japanese anarchist woman who happens to be a professor in Peace Studies, with one of her specialisms being on Errico Malatesta. Although the professor is not an Esperantist, she is nevertheless proficient in Italian and knows English. When I later contacted her, she told me that she did not remember Alexander very well, but she still received postcards and messages from him from time to time.

During that SAT Congress week in Belgrade, our good comrade Kani from the Spanish CNT arranged a meeting with the local group of the anarcho-syndicalist International Workers' Association. During the meeting, it seemed as if the Serbian comrades there already knew the name, Alexander Nakov.

On another occasion, as a further example of this, upon returning from one of the Congress workshops, I encountered a large, long-haired young man, dressed completely in black, who was waiting outside the entrance to the student hostel we were staying at. From his manner, he appeared to be in deep thought, and he looked as though he was looking for someone. So, I decided to speak to him. I asked him whether he was an anarchist and whom he was looking for. He said

Esperanto congress in Burgas, Bulgaria, July 16 1962.

that he was looking for Comrade Nakov.

This young man and I chatted at a nearby café as we waited for the others to arrive. As he was able to speak in English, David Kelso, then of the Scottish Esperanto Association, provided us with the necessary language support. It turned out that the young comrade, in some way, also had connections with the International Institute of Social History in Amsterdam.

Later, after returning home to Japan, I saw a number of websites which mentioned Alexander and rapidly came to the conclusion that he is definitely known, at least among certain sections of the anarchist movement.

After that, I picked up his book; then, by way of various comrades in Greece and Berkeley in the US, I eventually managed to get in touch with Mariya Radeva in Bulgaria, who immediately offered to translate Alexander's book into English. Meanwhile, I have known Rob Blow from the Anarchist Federation in Great Britain for many years, primarily as a comrade in SAT and its Libertarian Fraction. So when he agreed to take on the task of editing the book and looking

Alexander at the SAT worker Esperanto congress, in Belgrade, 2006

for an English language publisher, I knew we were already halfway there. The result of all this, you are now holding in your hands.

Viola M. Ando, October 2013

KOSACHA VILLAGE

BY ALEXANDER NAKOV

My native village is located 14 kilometres west of the town of Radomir, on the road to the village of Kovachevtsi. It is situated between the rounded and forested ridges of Cherna Gora Mountain[*] with its highest peak, Tumba, at 1129 metres. Kosacha adjoins the villages Kopanitsa, Radibosh, Kovachevtsi, Sirishtnik, Slatino, Kosturintsi and Planinitsa.

Kosacha is an old settlement with an old history. It received its name from the wife of Velimir, ruler of the Gradishte fortress. Her name was Kosacha. According to legend, the village was settled twice elsewhere before taking its current location. It was first settled in the Staro Selishte[†] area and later in the area called Selishte below the Gradishte fortress.

---

[*] Black Mountain.

[†] Staro Selishe translates as 'old settlement', while Selishe is simply 'settlement'.

At both sites one can see the remains of buildings.

During Ottoman rule, the village was an important junction. The two roads, Pazarski and Graovski, have both been preserved to this day and connect the Zemen and Treklian regions with Radomir, Pernik and Sofia.

As the village expanded, so did the herds. Pasture remained limited, causing whole extended families to migrate closer to the village common

My mother, Yordanka Khristova.

land. Our family, the Puevs, moved four kilometres away from the village centre, where they had previously lived, and settled in the picturesque area below Orlovitza* which was forested with centuries-old oaks in which eagles built their nests, hence the name.

Two leaders from Kosacha participated in the struggle against Ottoman rule in Macedonia. These were Marko Lazov, the son of Lazo Stoyanov, and Peter Ivanov Milev. Up to and during the 1903 uprising, Milev had been a revolutionary with Yane Sandanski.† He subsequenty became a leader in the Nevrokop revolutionary district, and was a supporter of Yane Sandanski. He was murdered on the night of July 9–10 1908 by enemies of the revolutionary movement in the village of Kovachevitsa in the Nevrokop region.

Two other revolutionaries were the brothers Georgi and Nikola Kostadinovi Gruevi. Nikola was murdered in an unknown location while his brother Georgi lived into his old age in the village of Barakovo in the Blagoevgrad region. The leader Marko Lazov lived into old age in Kosacha and was buried in the local cemetery there.

As with every other village at the end of the nineteenth

---

*Eagle's.

†1872–1915, Bulgarian-Macedonian left nationalist, leader of the Internal Macedonian-Adrianople Revolutionary Organization.

and the beginning of the twentieth centuries, life in Kosacha was bustling. During the period 1930–1944 the village was at its most populous with about 1200 residents and 180 houses. Each household had four to five children while families with six to eight members were not uncommon. The largest family had twelve children.

The population of the village remained around this level until 1946–1947. At the time, there was a 'youth cooperative' in the village with 72 members. This was dissolved by the Bolsheviks on the pretext that most of its members were anarchists who were conducting anarchist activity. That was when the gradual exodus from the village began.

My brother, Milcho Nakov.

The school in Kosacha was founded in 1843. Initially, it did not have a separate building and classes took place in private homes. The first teachers were Tsvetko Simeonov and Kuzman Nakov, both from Kosacha. According to information from the state archive in Pernik on the 1894-1895 school year, a total of 280 pupils attended the elementary school. In the first grade, the figure was 66 boys and 38 girls; second grade, 53 boys and 11 girls; third grade, 44 boys and 8 girls; fourth grade, 48 boys and 10 girls. By 1897, a total of 21 teachers were teaching at the school. Most of these were from Kosacha but some came from other places such as Radibosh, Kovchevtsi and Trekliano. The old elementary school, built in 1888, consisted of four rooms (two classrooms and two small rooms), with two larger rooms, added in 1921 thanks to the resources and labour of the villagers. The following residents of Kosacha contributed money to the cause: Iove Milev, 1300 lev*; Stoimen Georgiev, 1000 lev; Al. Mladenov, 500 lev; Zare Kostadinov, 500 lev; the priest Zahari Tonev, 500

*The Bulgarian unit of currency.

lev; Vele Stoianov, 500 lev; Mile Iovev, 500 lev; Zare Minev, 500 lev; Kote and Dimitar Velevi, 700 lev; Stoimen Bozhilov, 500 lev; and from another 122 people, 25,000 lev. The total of all these contributions was 34,000 lev.

Following the construction of the two new rooms, the school became the GS Rakovski Secondary School. It was the first secondary school in the region and pupils from the villages of Chepino, Svetlia, Sirishtnik, Kovachevtsi, Rakilov-tsi, Pchelintsi, Radibosh and Planinitsa studied in Kosacha. There was a 'hotel' for pupils from neighbouring villages – a room at the House of Culture was furnished with about 20 beds, so that when the weather was bad, they could spend the night there.

On account of the large number of pupils in the village, the school rooms were not big enough, so a new elementary school, Hristo Botev, was built in the Poliana neighborhood. I found archive data on the Hristo Botev School for the year 1940–1941 school year in which a total of 28 boys and 21 girls attended. In 1942–1943, a total of 40 pupils attended, 23 boys and 17 girls.

We also had a well-managed House of Culture named "Lazo Stoianov". When the Kosacha citizen Lazo Stoianov passed away, his son Georgi Lazarov donated to the village the 16 acres of fields he had inherited, with the wish that the dona-tion would go towards the construction of a House of Culture named after his father. A fund was created and a committee elected for the House of Culture's construction. The com-mittee included the donor Georgi Lazarov (Honorary Chair), Pavel Petrunov (Chair), Metodi Mladenov (Treasurer), the teacher, Vangelin Milanov (Secretary), with members Pavel Penev, Sergi Dimitrov, Aleksander D. Ortakchiiski, Dimitar Stoilov, Hristo Krastev and Rangel Z. Malinov.

The House of Culture was built with these donations with additionally collected funds and opened to the public in January 1927. The library was stocked with a rich collection of

The family of my brother Ivan: Stanka Metodieva, Milcho Metodiev, Vasil Metodiev and Ivan Metodiev.

literature and one of the first radio receivers in the Radomir region was housed at our House of Culture. Teachers were the driving force behind the cultural life in the village. They organized dance parties and talks on different topics, mostly on temperance. Acting troupes were also organized there. These went around the neighbouring villages and participated at national festivals, too. Both teachers and the progressive youth took part in all the village cultural events.

With the exception of a few families, people in the village lived poorly. Almost everyone was 'vegetarian'. They ate meat on St. George's Day, had lamb in the winter and pork at Christmas. Chicken was eaten when either the chicken or the owner of the chicken was ill. For the rest of the time, food was obtained from milk and its derivatives – butter, cheese, curds and buttermilk. Almost all the households had sheep and a goat or two. Bulls, cows and horses were used as draft animals for ploughing. Eggs were rarely eaten in the village but were sold or exchanged at the grocery shop for salt, matches, gas and sandals.

There was one wealthy man in the village, the merchant, Milen Lazov. He was the richest merchant in the town of Radomir. Later, however, he was cheated by his business partners and ended up as a beggar.

Many plum orchards had been planted near the village. From these, some of the produce was sold at the market in Pernik, other produce was bought by various merchants and the rest was used to make rakiya brandy. Later, a drying house was constructed to make prunes from the plums. This operated until the trees dried up. Our village was well known in the area for its fine aromatic pears of which there were over 40 varieties. These were sold at the markets in Pernik and Breznishko.

Many families could not live off their income from agriculture, so many of those people sought work at the Granitoid cement factory, the Batanovtsi train station or the Pernik coal mine.

With the World War II approaching, when the fascists and Bolsheviks were embracing each other like brothers, with the signing of the Ribbentrop-Molotov Pact on 23rd August 1939,[*] people became completely confused and life became less certain.

As I wrote elsewhere, only we, the anarchists, conducted the most active propaganda against the advancing brown plague from the West. The following village residents were imprisoned: Milcho Slavov Liubenov, Boyan Ivanov Vassev and myself, Alexander Nakov. There were also three partisans: Milcho Krumov, Yordan Mihalkov and Nikola G. Kovachki.[†] Later, when the Germans were already leaving, 17 volunteers from the village went after them to chase them away. Among these volunteers was my brother, Ivan Metodiev.

For a while after the coup of 9th September 1944,[‡] the Mayor of Kosacha was Ivan Ananiev, a former warder at Sofia Central

---

[*] More commonly known as the Hitler-Stalin Pact.

[†] These were, in fact, anarchist partisans.

[‡] Seizure of power by the Bolsheviks.

Prison. No one bothered us though, as at that point there were no local state representatives who were predisposed against anarchists. The new 'high up' authorities could not accept this situation. For them, it seemed an unforgivable sin that anarchists should remain undisturbed with their organized life and their propaganda. To get rid of us, the municipal authorities appointed their own Mayor 'from above'. He was from Pchelintsi village, although he had received his primary education in our village, and his name was Boris Pargov.

So, he turned out to be a good exec-utor of the tasks that the new author-ities had set him. He initiated heavy persecution of the anarchists. First he fired the teacher, Maria Doganova, and forced his former classmate, Milcho Slavov, to go and work as a teacher in Haskovo. While there, Milcho married a Komsomol* woman and began a life of 'peace and quiet'. The rest of the young people fled to the cities of Pernik, Sofia and elsewhere. In a short time the village was literally emptied of young people.

My sister, Pavlina.

After Pargov, the Bulgarian Com-munist Party (BCP) in Radomir appointed Stanko Gruev, a cobbler from the village, as Party Secretary and Mayor of the village. This man eagerly exercised the power granted him. He harassed the villagers with state collections of grain, meat, butter, etc. These collections were beyond the means of people and many began to flee to the cities in panic, mainly to Pernik and Sofia.

At some point, Stanko got sick and the Party sent him off for treatment at Aleksandrovska Hospital in Sofia. One of the villagers decided to 'thank' him for the harassment and sent the following telegram to his parents in Kosacha, signed as if

* Member of the Young Communists.

from his brother who worked on the Sofia tramways, 'Come immediately, Stanko has passed away!'

His younger brother, Gruyo, reported the telegram to the Party's Regional Committee and they immediately provided an automobile to bring home the honoured activist, Stanko.

Arriving at the hospital, Gruyo found his brother sitting up in bed. He told him about the telegram and called his parents and relatives in Kosacha, who were preparing the funeral. They, however, did not believe that Stanko was alive. He had to be brought from the hospital to the village by car so they could see that he was still alive. He was then returned to the hospital.

While the villagers thought that Stanko had died, they made merry all night in the pubs. The next day, when they discovered that he had not actually died, they drank all night, but this time from sorrow.

When he returned to the village, Stanko became even more nasty and vengeful and began using the power granted him to take revenge on his fellow villagers. When someone needed a letter of recommendation for work or a reference, he presented the person in the darkest colours. This was the real face of this empowered nonentity.

The agricultural cooperative is not a Bolshevik creation. The villagers had long been convinced that salvation lay in the collective tilling of the soil. Before 9th September 1944, despite the opposition of bourgeois power, 29 well-organized agricultural cooperatives existed in the country, cultivating their land in unison. There was also a Cooperative Bank, as well as many consumer cooperatives. There was one such consumer cooperative in Kosacha. Only one person there received a salary and goods were sold much more cheaply than at the grocery. But instead of providing an opportunity for this movement to flourish, the Bolsheviks forced people to join their collective farms. A collective farm was formed in Kosacha in 1956. In 1957 this was expanded. Only a few people, six or seven persons, had the courage not to join it. Most villagers were press-ganged into working for 30 stotinkas per day.*

One fellow from the village, Stamen Velikov, an uncle of President Georgi Parvanov,† decided to hide a goat and two kids from this 'cooperative' by taking them to Pernik, where he worked. When the Mayor found out about this outrage, he decided to return what had been hidden from the People's State. He sent a cooperative farm member to bring the goat and kids in to the collective farm. He gave the man a horse and the man rode the horse straight to some crooks in Pernik. He placed the kids in the saddlebags, tied a rope around the goat's neck and rode off to Kosacha to the collective farm. Kosacha, however, is twenty kilometres away. So, it was curtains for the goat after being virtually throttled, and the kids were eaten, too. Thus, it all ended well. There was no doubt of what awaited anyone who questioned the strength and justice of the People's State.

The collective farm demanded a certain number of working days each month to be provided by everyone conscripted into it. If a person skipped work, he was deprived of goods and length of service for retirement. At this time I was employed at the Republic mine in Pernik and on my days off I used to go to the village. My mother, who was generally frail, asked me to join the collective farm brigades to make up her missed work days. Later, my brother's children worked instead of their grandmother, but for them, the Brigade Leader wrote down only half a workday.

At first, people worked in the hope that their labour would become easier and their income, as promised, would increase. When they realized that any benefits were going only to those at the top of the hierarchy, those who get the lion's share, then, on the quiet, people began to spin out their work.

---

*1 stotinka = one hundredth of a Bulgarian lev.

†In office 2002–2012.

Here's a comical example, where 'three are looking for two'. One day, a youth who had delivered a cartload of hay for the sheep at the farm told the Brigade Leader, 'I got tired loading the hay. Now find some other people to unload it.' So the Brigade Leader, the Mayor and the Party Secretary all went traipsing around the village to find two people to unload the hay from the cart.

The collective farms were created in a criminal manner, and they were shut down in an equally criminal way. Fear was the only stimulus. Slogans like, 'The first sheaves go to the state' inspired nobody. People understood that the biggest bandit, the state, was robbing and stealing from them. Finally, the collective farm had to join an agro-industrial complex centered in the municipality of Kovachevtsi. A busload of civil servants had to be brought in from Pernik every day, as sufficient people could no longer be found to work in the fields. Brigades mobilized from factories in Pernik and Radomir were not enough to help with the labour shortage.

When ripened socialism grew overripe and rotted, when Zhelev* became concerned that the love of the people might harm the glory of the Bolsheviks, he started to preach the 'velvet revolution.' This velvet revolution was used by the nomenklatura† to quickly make a grab for halfpennies and farm machinery. Commissions were set up to liquidate the cooperatives. The people's land was to be returned, with actual boundaries. Nobody asked them how they wanted to manage the land that was to be returned to them; whether they wanted to work it as a cooperative, an association, or individually. The situation had become such that the villagers no longer possessed animals, stock or equipment, and most importantly, there were no longer people capable of carrying out the work. It was not possible to return to the age of the plough, so as a result, almost all of the fertile land was

---

* Zhelyu Zhelev, the first post-Bolshevik President, 1992-1997.

†Party bureaucrats and privileged elements in the former Soviet Union and Eastern Bloc.

abandoned.

Prior to the collective farm's formation, there were over 10,000 sheep and goats and about 450 head of cattle. The collective farm organized four flocks of sheep with about 1,200 sheep in each. The rest of the animals disappeared somewhere. Following the farm's 'liquidation,' in the early 1990s* there were only about 200 sheep and goats and about 20 cows left in the village.

My wife, Kirilka Aleksieva.

Salvation rested in cooperation, not in collective farms and not in individual cultivation. Since the stock had been stolen and since people had no means to restock, we now see only deserted land. There were no people, no animals and no hope to restore what had been lost.

Because there were no young people left in the village, demographic collapse followed. The school rooms gradually emptied. The first school to close and be demolished was Hristo Botev in the Poliana neighborhood. Soon after, the G. S. Rakovski Secondary School was closed. That was in 1965-1966. Later, in 1973, the primary school closed, too. Today, no trace is left of the two schools and the House of Culture. They have been razed to the ground. The big elm tree still stands in the yard to remind those still alive how we climbed on it during our PE lessons. The only building left is the church, which has been renovated and fenced off. But there, too, nobody enters. There are about 100 people left in the village, but these are just the elderly who rely predominantly on their pensions. Before the Bolshevik coup, about 1200 people used to live in the village. According to the 1934 census, there were 1026 people in the village; in 1946, 917 people; in 1956, 603 people;

* This was a typographical error in the Bulgarian original, which said the year "1900."

in 1979, 280 people; and in 2008, 103 people.

Today in the whole of the Kovachevtsi municipality, in the village of Sirnishtik to be precise, there is one single school left for grades 1 to 8 with 20 students and 5 teachers.

In 1984 a service building was erected for the needs of the village. It contains the Town Hall, the store, the pub and a room where the books left over from the library are kept. The water supply, after many delays, was installed for part of the village, mainly in the center. There is even water in the graveyard now, an initiative of Deputy Mayors since the changes of 1989.

In 1934, labourers built the section of the road that now connects Radomir and Kosacha. Later, a section was built through the village of Liaskovets as a shortcut to Pernik and Sofia. Subsequently, because Kovachevtsi was the home village of the "leader and teacher", Dimitrov*, the road was widened and asphalted to provide a convenient connection with Pernik and the capital, as well as with the other areas in the region.

In conclusion, I can say that we now have roads but no schools or Houses of Culture. Virtually all of the villages have been almost or completely depopulated. In a neighboring village, Kosturintsi, which was well populated in the past, only two people are left there today. It is said that those two residents do not even speak to each other. This is what we have inherited from the "centenarians"† – at least in our part of the country.

---

*Georgi Dimitrov Mikhailov, 1882-1949, first Bolshevik leader of post-war Bulgaria.

†Nickname of the Bulgarian Socialist Party.

INDEX

Persons

Achanov, Dimiter Vasilev 5.
Agontseva, Raina 8.
Aleksandrov, Boyan 'The Granny' 5, 80.
Aleksov, Bogdan 4.
Aleksov, Boyan 4, 10, 12, 17, 33, 39, 63, 66, 80, 93.
Alexev, Boyan xxiii.
Alito (Chief Post Officer) 75.
Andonov, Vladimir xxiv.
Ando, Viola M. 122, 124.
Anka Menkovi 31.
Apostolski, Mikhail 16, 23.
Arnaudov, Kiril Kunev (aka Kiril Gaberov) 5, 12, 13.
Arshinov,Pyotr x.
'Auntie' Milka 2.
Bakunin, Mikhail vii, x.
Balev, Dr. Ivan 78.
Balkanski, Georgi (aka Georgi Grigoriev) vii.
Balkhov, Dimitar vii.
Baltov, Ivan 66.
Baramov, Todor xxiv.
Barev, Tsenko 14.
Barzakov, Lyuben 114.
Blow, Rob vi, xiii, xvii, 112, 114, 123.
Bogdanov, Boris 46.
Boichev, Hristo 87, 88.
Bonev, Radi 79.
Boris III, King of Bulgaria ix.
Borisov, Yordan xxiii.
Boshov, Slavcho 11.

Botev, Hristo vii, 19, 58, 112, 128, 135.
Bozhanata, Todor Angelov 9.
Bozhilov, George Yordanov 4.
Bozhilov, Krum 75.
Bozhilov, Stoimen 128.
Bretanov, Dimitur 82.
Chicago Martyrs 112.
Cyril (Saint) 47.
Damianov, Gancho Lazarov 8, 84, 85, 86, 88, 89, 90.
Dancho. *See* Yordan (Dancho).
Dimitrov, Alexander 11.
Dimitrov, Boris 15.
Dimitrov, Dimitur 88.
Dimitrov, George Mihov 13.
Dimitrov, Georgi 48.
Dimitrov, Metodi 4.
Dimitrov, Peter 4.
Dimitrov, Sergi 128.
Dimitrov, Stamen 4.
Dimitrov, Stamenko 93.
Dimitrov, Stanke xxiii.
Dimov, Maksim 79.
Dimov,Milen 64.
Dobridolski, Yancho 18.
Doganova, Maria 32, 39, 44, 131.
Draganova, Tsvetana 44.
Drenchev, Milan 47, 48.
Dr. Momchilova 74.
Drundov, Ivan 11.
Duganova, Maria xxiii.
Duparanov, Vasil 64.

666666666666666

Places

Publications

Sundry (organizations, institutions, movements, etc.) xix.